PLAYING THE
WEALTH
GAME

PLAYING THE
WEALTH
GAME

THE STRATEGIES BEHIND FINANCIAL MOVES THAT WIN

FREDDIE RAPPINA
ChFC® RICP® AIF® CLU® CCFS®

DEDICATION

I dedicate this book to my awesome wife, Barbara, our children Rylin and Penelope. Together, we've forged a Chess-playing family, enabling us to cherish vital aspects of life, like competitive travel baseball and cheerleading. I also extend this dedication to my parents, Fred and Phyllis, and my in-laws, Larry and Kathy, who are relishing their retirements after mastering a great game of Checkers.

CONTENTS

In order to improve your game, you must study
the endgame before everything else.

—José Capablanca

INTRODUCTION

The man who sat across from me in my office had done everything "right." He'd maxed out his 401k. He'd contributed to an IRA. He had paid off his house. He had a six-month emergency fund. And yet, as retirement approached, he began to wonder, "Is this it? This is all I have to look forward to?"

Because as we sat there and did the math, he began to get a clearer picture of his retirement years. His belief was that being committed to saving meant he'd have enough money to take a vacation each year with his wife. He could help his eldest go back to school. He'd still have a little left over to rent a cabin on the lake in the summers.

"I expected more out of retirement, to be honest," he said. "I didn't expect to be on a private island, but I had hoped that with all this free time, I could afford to take all those trips we put off. We wanted to buy a house in Florida and retire there, maybe even get a boat to take out in Tampa Bay. It doesn't look like I'll be able to do all that."

I meet dozens of people who have worked hard all their lives, made pretty decent money, and envisioned retirement as the time when they could enjoy the fruits of their labors. Then all those missed soccer games and lunches at their desk would be worth the sacrifice. They don't expect to buy their own Lear jet with their investments; they simply want to have a higher degree of financial freedom.

As a side note, I'm using many financial terms more colloquially, because this isn't a book for financial advisors. It's for everyday people, like this client, like you, who want to learn the strategies of the wealthy. You don't need a lot of fancy words to do that. But you do need a plan, if you want the next phase of your life to be more than you imagined.

If you have a million dollars in your 401k and start drawing 4% of the balance each year to fund your retirement, that means you now have $40,000 of generally taxable income coming in each year. The idea is to be in a lower tax bracket than you were when you were employed so you don't get hammered by taxes. But who wants to cut back on their life when they retire? It seems completely counterintuitive to pare down when you finally have the time to enjoy what you worked so hard to achieve.

Essentially, you've played a really good game of Checkers with your money, and while you are probably in a much better financial position than the majority of people who only have a tenth of that amount in their 401k, you may want just a bit more.

By changing the game you play, you can change the outcome. I've helped many people make Chess moves with their money, teaching them the strategies I have used to build my own wealth. They have learned how to make taxes work for, instead of against, them, how to use real estate to create the ultimate checkmate, and how to leave their kids with the financial freedom to pursue their passions.

This book is designed to teach you the same thing. This book is a self-discovery style book, designed to help you figure out if you'd rather play Checkers or Chess as you're making financial moves. By the end, you should know whether you are a Chess or Checkers player right now and whether you want to change your game. That doesn't mean everyone has to play Chess; quite the contrary. There is absolutely nothing wrong with playing Checkers with your money—just make sure you are playing the best possible Checkers game so you can achieve the best possible results.

But if you want to put a little more risk on the table and make strategic moves that build your wealth in your sleep, then Chess may be the game for you. Just like in real life with the checkerboard, you learn these tactics a little at a time, making small moves that eventually become big ones.

No matter which game you choose to play, this book will help teach you to play it well. You'll have money moves you can use to make your retirement fit the ideal you pictured all those times you sat in rush-hour traffic. I'm a former Checkers player who has converted to Chess. I've used the same strategies in this book and am here to teach you how to up your own game to improve your results, a little, or a lot.

Or you might just end up like the guy on Star Island, who unwittingly became the light bulb moment for me that changed everything about how I approach wealth and value. That's a story for another chapter.

For now, let's start playing the game better than you ever have before.

"Tactics is knowing what to do when there is something to do. Strategy is knowing what to do when there is nothing to do."

– Garry Kasparov

FIRST, UNDERSTAND THE GAME YOU'RE PLAYING

Deep in Central Park (and just a few miles from the Wall Street trading floor), there's an octagonal brick building called the Chess and Checkers House. Since 1952, people have been coming to this little red-and-cream structure to pick out a checkerboard and then choose which game they are going to play: Chess or Checkers.

One is a game of knowledge, planning, deep thought, and strategic moves. The other is simpler, less strategic, and more accessible to anyone interested in playing a game. With both games, you have the potential to lose as much as you do to win; it's all in how you play the game.

To me, the game of building wealth works a lot like Chess and Checkers. You can play either game at an amateur level or, by working with people who truly understand the strategies I'm going to lay out in this book, at an expert level. It doesn't require a degree in finance, either. It's all about changing the way you look at money, debt, and taxes. In case you didn't know, taxes can be your friend. We'll get to how in a second.

I'm a wealth advisor and see people every day who have the same goal: to grow their money and make it work for them, instead of working to earn that money until the day they die. There are people who walk into my office and choose Checkers and others who are eager to play Chess. Neither one of them is right or wrong in their choice as long as they are informed about what they are doing and why they are making that choice. Knowing which game you are playing is vital if you're going to play either game well—and win.

That's the key: Play whichever game you choose as well as you can because that's how you make a big difference in your financial future. Maybe you want to retire on a private island, or maybe you just want a nice house near the grandkids. The future most of us desire is usually framed by one constant—financial confidence. No one wants to worry about running out of money at eighty or being bankrupted by a stay in a rehab facility. The reality is that many of us will end up that way if we don't play a better game with our money.

Don't think that will be you? Here's a startling, and sadly true, fact: Nearly half of all Americans have saved *nothing* toward retirement.[1]

Not a dime.

Maybe they're waiting on a rich uncle to die and leave them a few million, which is very unlikely to happen to the vast majority of people. Even those who have contributed to their 401k or other retirement plan aren't in very good shape. "As of the end of 2022, the average 55 to 64-year-old's 401(k) is worth $207,874," said a recent CNN.com article.[2] If you're in that group, you might dread the day you stop working or constantly worry about how you'll pay your bills.

Wouldn't it be fabulous to have a solid financial future where you know you'll be more than comfortably well off and, moreover, be able to build generational wealth for your kids and grandkids, gifting them with the same solid future? You can do that if you begin to play Chess. While it's not impossible to do solely by playing a great game of Checkers with your money, it's a lot more difficult.

The problem is that most people are sold a game of Checkers by a lot of financial advisors or financial pundits but are being told that they're playing Chess. They're not. Chess and Checkers have two totally different ways of approaching

---

1 https://usafacts.org/data-projects/retirement-savings

2 https://www.cnn.com/cnn-underscored/money/average-401k-balance-by-age

wealth, and as you move from one game to the other, you can use the lessons you learned to play either game better and get better results.

Let's talk about the difference in the two games and the average players for each. Chances are you fall into one of these two categories, or maybe you're somewhere in the middle. This book is designed to help you figure out what game you are playing, whether you want to change your game, how to play Chess or Checkers strategically, and how to take your wealth game to the next level.

I want to preface this by saying loud and clear:

> There is nothing wrong with being a Checkers or Chess player. What works for you is what works for you. Just as there is no one tool for building wealth, there is no one right answer for *your* money.

CHECKERS PLAYERS

Checkers players (side note: everything I'm about to say is a general description; your mileage can, and probably does, vary) look at money differently than Chess players do. For many Checkers players, the word *wealth* makes them uncomfortable. They were raised with the idea that money is the root of all evil, so they see wanting too much as a bad thing. They don't want to be greedy or live a life of consumer consumption. They definitely don't want to live like the Kardashians. Their goal is not necessarily to be financially independent, but rather to be happy.

Here's the thing—those two states of being are not mutually exclusive. You can be financially independent, wealthy even, and still be happy. We'll get to that more in a minute.

Checkers players are usually the children of Checkers players who worked a job for thirty years, then received a pension and a gold watch when they retired. They believe in the value of hard work. They believe giving their kids money will spoil them (although there is a difference between giving your kids money and giving your kids *opportunities* through money). They often sit on their money and save it for a rainy day or just keep saving and not spending it, like the sixty-five-year-old retired firefighter who came in to see me.

He had $2 million in his retirement account. I asked him what he wanted to do with the money. "Save it," he said. "When I'm seventy-five, I hope to have four million."

But, I reasoned, then he'd be ten years older and have ten less years to enjoy that money, so why wait to put it to use? Why sit on the sidelines watching it grow when he could be living possibly a better lifestyle right now, while he's still on earth and physically able to enjoy it?

He hesitated because he was a Checkers player and was nervous about taking a risk, which is totally okay. Many people feel that way, and that's great if that works for them. I'm not here to browbeat you into choosing a game of Chess. I simply want you to understand where you are now and where that plan will take you.

For the most part, Checkers players are savers who favor 401k plans, IRAs, CDs, mutual funds, or pensions. Checkers players have a budget, a checklist, and a standard retirement account. They've been listening to the financial pundits say, "This is the best way to save." Checkers players may not be financially savvy, and they may not want to be financially savvy. They simply want to make enough money to retire and live comfortably. They also tend to have several misconceptions about concepts like taxes and compound interest, something we'll discuss later in this book.

Again, I'm not saying Checkers players are bad people or that they're making dumb mistakes. The vast majority are trying to make careful money decisions that they hope will pay off well in the end. They likely won't be wealthy but they will be financially secure, which is great. Checkers players don't need to reach for a bigger and better game if they don't want to; they just need to be clear on the fact that they are playing Checkers, not Chess.

> You can have a great life as a Checkers player. You can be extremely happy, comfortable, and leave a little to the kids.

Good Checkers players don't exactly live paycheck to paycheck, but they're often very close to the edge of a financial disaster and end up working longer to try to save more. Less than a third of all Americans have more than six months of bills saved[3], which means if they lost their job tomorrow, they'd need to find a new one pretty quickly or they could be out on the street.

Good Checkers players start off by being debt-free so they aren't panicked if they hit a bump in the road. Here's the truth: If you're going to play Checkers, you need to be damn good at it. Nothing sucks more in any economy than being a bad Checkers player.

Checkers players often find that they reach their fifties or sixties and the life they dreamed of in their twenties isn't the reality they are living. They earn six figures, but it's not giving them the lifestyle they thought it would. So, they work longer hours trying to make even more, continually playing catchup but never quite reaching the brass ring.

---

3 https://www.fool.com/the-ascent/banks/articles/only-27-of-americans-have-enough-savings-to-cover-more-than-6-months-of-living-expenses/

> Checkers players may think the only way to make more money is to trade more time.

The reality is that your time is valuable, and each day that ticks by eats away a little more of the time you have left. Like the firefighter who came to see me, I believe you have a choice between watching the money grow or letting the money start working for you right now so you don't have to work an extra ten or twenty years to live the life you dreamed of. Wouldn't you prefer to spend *today* enjoying the fruits of your labor rather than waiting until some vague tomorrow? If so, maybe Chess is the game for you.

CHESS PLAYERS

Chess players see money as a necessary tool to get them where they want to go. Their mindset about almost everything related to their finances is different than Checkers players. They see beyond 401k plans and whether it's better to choose Roth or traditional IRAs. They look at market investments and diversify their assets by investing in stocks, bonds, real estate, businesses, crypto currency, etc., as ways to expand their financial position and then plan how to use that as the greatest weapon in their wealth-building arsenal.

> Money doesn't buy happiness, that is true. But it does put a down payment on it.

Chess players tend to think of businesses and investments as projects, not as weights holding them down. Once they make this one work, they move on to the next project. They don't feel constrained by one type of business or one direction of thinking. They don't feel stuck. They see *possibility* and use those possibilities to move into bigger and better directions, ones that may or may not even be related to each other. There are commonalities in the choices that Chess players make; however, that I'll get to in a later chapter, and it may not be what you think.

Elon Musk, for instance, created PayPal, a third-party method of sending people money. He didn't stay stuck in the world of payment methods, instead he moved on to electric cars and sending rocket ships to Mars. Those types of companies aren't even remotely related by anything other than the fact that Musk thought: *What if?*

Chess players aren't focused on accumulating wealth; for them, it's not about the money. What? How can that be? But no, it's true. They aren't watching the dollars add up, instead they look at what those dollars mean to their lives. They are focused on the two things that wealth can give them: Time and freedom. They'll change direction on a dime if something isn't working out for them and move on to something else. They'll

15

give up on something if it is becoming more of a hindrance than a growth opportunity or taking up more time than they want to give.

I get it that you're probably reading this and thinking, *Only rich people say crap like that. It's only after you have the wealth to cover your lifestyle that people say it's not about the money.*

If you're living paycheck to paycheck and struggling to pay the bills, then it definitely feels like it's all about the money. I get it. I've been there. I was a police officer in Fairfax County, which is a suburb of Washington, DC, and I watched every single dime of every single paycheck. But wouldn't it be great if it wasn't all about the money all the time? If you weren't freaking out every time the last day of the month rolled around?

A Checkers player will look at their bank account and think, *What should I do?* A Chess player can look at those same numbers and think, *What can I do differently?*

That's the singular mindset difference between the two, and it can make a massive difference in the moves you make with your money—and the results you see. A Chess mindset is all about getting more time, not more money. They look at how they can make the current situation work for them and scale it to become even better. Instead of thinking they'll never be as rich as Musk so why bother, they think: If someone else has been super, super successful, that means I can be successful too. That also means I can have more time to spend with my family, travel the world, build wells in Africa…whatever the

Chess player has dreamed of doing with those hours he or she isn't punching in and out.

Chess players don't feel compelled to play the game on a Bezos or Buffett level. They can play it at a level where they feel comfortable and still accumulate enough wealth to create that lifestyle they dreamed of in their twenties. They can build enough wealth to have the time to actually enjoy their money.

> **Chess players are more concerned with compounding their lifestyle than interest.**

Again, there is nothing wrong with playing Checkers versus Chess if that's what makes you feel happy and content. When I was early in my career with the police department, I was a Checkers player. I was always working overtime to try to put some money in my savings, but it cost me time with the people who were most important to me. I saw those extra hours, and the stress they brought with them, affecting the joy I had in my job and in my off hours. I looked at the price I was paying in my relationships (and my happiness) and thought there had to be a better way. That's what led me to start studying finance and learning how the game was played.

I started by learning everything I could about Checkers. Then I had a light bulb moment that showed me Chess can be an even more satisfying (and lucrative) game to play. I realized I didn't have to follow the same path as everyone else. I could carve out my own and create the life I always wanted. I just had to be bold enough to switch the game I played.

A lot of times, people (like me in those days) choose to play Checkers because they think it's a lower-risk proposition. To me, Checkers is the *highest risk* game to play. Why? Because, when you're relying on your day job to fund your life and future and you get laid off, your income is suddenly zero. That future is gone, and your day-to-day just got a lot more stressful.

Savings accounts have been touted as a safe way to add to what you put aside. What most people don't realize is: If you put your money in the bank to grow, you're looking at a borderline guaranteed way to lose money. Why? Because inflation will beat you time and time again. The inflation rate is *significantly* higher than the APY most savings accounts deliver. The average inflation rate, just in a normal year with no pandemics, product shortages, or wars, is 2-3%.[4] The national average APY (Annual Percentage Yield) of a savings account is a whopping 0.6%. That's not even half of what inflation costs you. The inflation rate in 2023 and 2024 was even higher, and though you might have been receiving 4-5% APY on your savings account, it's still not enough to keep up with the rate of inflation.

Then there's the stock market, which most people know can be very volatile and might not be the best place for all of your

---

4 https://www.investopedia.com/inflation-rate-by-year-7253832

money. If you're only investing in the market and the market crashes, you could lose your retirement overnight. With the market, your financial future is in the hands of other people, not yours.

These are standard Checkers moves—and while they aren't bad, they aren't great—and, in some cases, could cost you more than you are making. They aren't bad from the standpoint that you could be doing something worse for your financial future. Yet people keep choosing to play Checkers because they think it's safer. The truth is they are likely drowning in the shallow end and somehow thinking that's less risky, while the Chess players are diving into the deep end and looking for the best water for swimming further.

CHESS ISN'T ROCKET SCIENCE

It's true. To play Chess effectively you do have to have some financial knowledge. If you don't gain the knowledge you need, you risk playing badly and overleveraging yourself. You can't just fund a Chess game like you fund a 401k. There are strategic moves you need to be able to make—and you must understand *why* you are making those moves, which is what this book is all about. It's going to take you through different possible decisions and give you both the upside and the downside.

In reality, you don't need a Mensa-level IQ to play Chess. Anyone can do it if they have the right mindset, take the time to understand finance, and partner with a team that is playing on the same kind of board. I learned it, I've taught it to my clients, and this book is here to give you a head start on playing a great game.

IS CHECKERS MAKING YOU HAPPY?

Many people play Checkers, do just fine, and have enough money to live comfortably. To play Checkers well, however, you have to have all the pieces in place: An emergency fund, college funds, life insurance, and retirement accounts.

The problem is a lot of Checkers players work at jobs that they don't really love, put in hours that don't make them happy, and struggle to put enough aside to someday leave that job. I don't know about you, but that kind of life certainly didn't bring me joy. I see that same feeling in so many people I meet.

I remember dealing with someone at the DMV who was being really rude to me. Instead of barking back, I became super nice. At the end of the meeting, she apologized for being short with me.

I said, "I get it. This probably wasn't your dream job when you were growing up and it's tough to come in here day after day." She got a little misty-eyed because those words hit home. Simply acknowledging that I understood her situation made her feel seen and appreciated.

> Advertising has us chasing cars and clothes, working jobs we hate so we can buy shit we don't need. (I first heard that quote in *Fight Club*, but we don't talk about *Fight Club*.)

If you're still clocking in and out and hoping you can become wealthy by working enough hours, the truth is it probably won't happen. It's very, *very* difficult to become wealthy just by playing Checkers because you simply don't have enough pieces on the board to make the moves to take you to the next level. So, if you want to spend your retirement not stressing about whether Social Security is still going to be there, then you might want to up your game.

Forty years ago, people could work for the same employer for thirty years, retire, and live off a healthy pension. You knew you wouldn't be completely wealthy, but you wouldn't be completely broke either. That money was always going to be there and was a nice addition to Social Security.

These days, pensions are not what they used to be—if employers offer one at all—and the idea of working at the same company for thirty years is almost laughable. Most workers, in fact, stay less than ten years at the same company.[5] The world has changed and many retirements are now self-funded.

---

5 https://www.bls.gov/news.release/tenure.nr0.htm

On top of that, if you're living paycheck to paycheck you're likely not maxing out that retirement plan or investing in other opportunities. That means most people have barely enough to cover their living expenses when they retire, never mind affording things like long-term care or a lengthy hospitalization.

A 2019 study by the Employee Benefit Research Institute found that the average person in their early sixties with a household income of $71,000 to $126,000 has only saved about $150,000 in their retirement accounts. Those who are making more than $125,000 a year have about a half a million dollars saved.[6]

Is that enough to pay for living until you're eighty (especially when the average couple pays $300,000-plus for long-term care)? Probably not. While a half a million sounds like a lot of money, it goes quickly with rising expenses (don't forget our old friend inflation, which makes prices rise a little every year). That doesn't leave much for those trips you planned when you were working sixty-hour weeks and missing the kids' soccer games. The life you envisioned when you started socking money away in a 401k or IRA dwindles with each withdrawal.

Think of your 401k like an old, deep water well. Each year, you contribute to this well by pouring in buckets of water (your

---

6 https://www.ebri.org/docs/default-source/ebri-issue-brief/ebri_
   ib_562_401k-long-30june22.pdf?sfvrsn=f36d382f_8

investments). Over time, the water level rises, representing the growth of your investments as you continue to contribute and benefit from compound interest.

When you start drawing water out of the well in retirement, the sequence of return risk comes into play. If you hit a series of years with poor investment returns early on in your retirement, it's akin to dealing with a drought that makes the water level in your well drop significantly. You're now drawing water from a shallower well, which means you might run out of water much sooner than you expected.

Conversely, if you experience strong investment returns in the early years of your retirement, your well might fill to the brim, maybe even spill over the edge. You can draw from it without worrying too much about running out.

This analogy demonstrates that the order of investment returns matters. If you experience poor returns early on in retirement— even if the market improves later—you might not have enough left in your 401k to take advantage of the recovery. This is why asset allocation, diversification, and planning for the sequence of returns are so important when managing your retirement investments.

A lot of Checkers players go through each day hoping and praying they can avoid a drought, which is pretty much impossible. Bad years happen to all of us. Markets take dips all the time.

Many Checkers players might be hoping for that one big (and probably unlikely) payday, maybe from the lottery. That's why the Powerball is so popular—millions of people are hoping to be that one-in-a-gazillion person who wins a ton of money and is set for life. Statistically, your chances of winning the Powerball are 1 in 292.2 million[7]. You are more likely to die from a bee sting (a 1 in 57,822 chance), be eaten by a shark (1 in 3.25 million), or be struck by lightning (a 1 in 1,222,000 chance) than win a mega jackpot. The lottery is for people who are bad at math because those numbers aren't even remotely in their favor.

THE BEST ANSWER ISN'T AN ANSWER

There is no one answer to financial freedom. There is only the answer that is right for *you*. Your risk tolerance level, your goals, your lifestyle. You'll hear financial pundits call one financial tool bad or another one good (they'll say things like don't do this; only do that). Those kinds of clickbait headlines are too black-and-white for me.

The financial tools you use can be complex and flexible at the same time. Some work better than others for the situation you are in at this moment in time. Some will work well now but won't be the right choice down the road, and others will be a great option when you have mastered a few Chess moves.

---

7 https://www.investopedia.com/managing-wealth/worth-playing-lottery/

It's all about understanding *how* the tool you are using works and whether you have the right tool for the right goal, just like when you're doing some home remodeling. A wrench itself isn't a bad tool. However, if you're trying to nail a bracket onto the wall, a hammer is clearly the better tool for the job. There's nothing wrong with the wrench itself; it's simply not what you need right now. There are too many so-called advisors running around trying to sell wrenches to their clients as if they were hammers.

> **People are always looking for that one product that will make them wealthy.**

I'll say it again: There is no product out there that is guaranteed to do that, and if you're hoping this book will give you the secret recipe, you might as well stop reading. If there was one answer for wealth, everyone would buy into it. Every financial tool has pluses and minuses, and every financial tool comes with a certain degree of risk. Building wealth has more to do with strategies than products.

Don't just focus on the wealth you are building—knowing where your happiness level lies is far more important. Lots of people in finance will ask you what you do for work, how much money you have saved, how much you want to invest, etc., but they rarely ask: *What makes you happy?*

If that answer is having time to spend with your kids or enough money to go to Paris for a month, then that's what you should shoot for. If your answer is enough money to have freedom of choice and time to make those choices, keep reading.

"...Strategy is seeing the outcome of slow maneuvers, and also anticipating what you can do to disturb your opponent's plans."

– Garry Kasparov

CHAPTER TWO

RETIREMENT SHOULD BE MORE THAN A GOLD WATCH

As I mentioned in the last chapter, if you're one of those people who doesn't have much saved for retirement, then these pages should be a reality check for you. You need to know your numbers to know what your future will look like, and that means taking a minute to examine where you are today and where you want to be tomorrow.

So many of us dream of that day when we hand in our keys to the office, have a slice of cake in the breakroom, and walk out of the building for good while putting on the "I'm retired" T-shirt and spending our afternoons doing anything besides working. But are we dreaming big enough or early enough? I don't think so, which is why so many people reach those years and are disappointed by where they are financially.

The biggest problem with retirement is that people don't think about it until it's almost too late. When you're in your twenties, fresh out of college and worried about making rent, sixty-five seems really far away. You're focused on the here-and-now, not the down-the-road. To think about your financial future means actually pausing for a minute and imagining the next forty years.

- Do you still want to be working this kind of job when you're thirty? Forty? Fifty? Sixty?
- Would you rather have the time and freedom to explore a passion of yours?
- Do you want to retire at sixty-five or sixty-seven? Or at fifty-five? Forty-seven?

If you want to retire well and possibly even young, then you're going to need money. Money gives you opportunities. Money gives you choices. When you don't have money, you don't have a lot of choices—and frankly, that sucks. If you can figure out these concepts early, you can make the shifts you need to get you closer to where you want to be today, tomorrow, and years from now. So, how are we going to put a little (or a lot) of gas into your financial freedom engine and get it speeding down the road? By thinking strategically.

START ENVISIONING WHAT YOU WANT

When you're focused on the bills in front of you right now, you're missing the big picture. When envisioning the future you want, being specific about those dreams helps your mind focus on attaining that dream.

> People aren't achieving their dreams because they're not taking the time to envision those dreams in the first place.

I want you to think big, but not about possessions and material things. While it's awesome to own your own private island and have a jet to get back and forth, is that really what's important to you? Or would you like to have enough money to visit your grandkids whenever you want? To travel with your spouse? To help your child start a business?

Like I said in Chapter One, it's not just about things—it's about the *lifestyle* you want to live. That lifestyle is full of doing what you want...whatever you dream of doing. It doesn't matter whether that's visiting every country in the world or painting landscapes. What would make you happy and fulfilled?

These aren't just rhetorical questions. They're ones you should pause and answer right now because knowing that information will very likely influence the choices you make after reading this book.

In my opinion, too many people's dreams aren't big enough or grand enough. Maybe they're afraid to dream that big or already resigned to never achieving the kind of wealth that would help them achieve their big dreams. There's a difference between being realistic and selling yourself short. You may not be wealthy enough to own your own island (or even want to own an island) but that doesn't mean you can't make enough money to go to whatever island you want, whenever you want.

I think these caution flags started because our vision of retirement is skewed. Most people see retirement as an end game. I work this many years, I hand in my notice, and I...do what? They aren't thinking about life *after* retirement. They're only looking at the years it's going to take to get there. It's a destination instead of a strategic, well-thought-out plan.

So, stop right here. Imagine your life after retirement in the context of financial freedom, whether that retirement comes in your sixties or your thirties. Where do you live? What are you doing day to day? Who do you spend time with? Are you traveling? Jetting off someplace warm in the winter? How are you living off the fruits of your labor (and hopefully still receiving lots of passive income)? Take a second to dream of this future and write it down. This can help shift your mindset from retirement being a destination to it being a fulfillable dream.

It's not really our fault we look at retirement this way. We've been taught to have that kind of end-game vision since we were kids. When you first went to school, it was all about getting to the next grade. When you get to high school, all you can think about is getting to senior year and graduating. Then, getting through four years (or more) of college and being done with school. Then getting a job. Buying a house. Saving money. Retiring. End of journey. All of those milestones symbolize "one day." *One day, I'll graduate high school. One day, I'll live in my own apartment. One day, I'll start my career.*

And the big one: *One day, I'll retire.*

I despise the whole "one day" viewpoint. How can you make your financial freedom happen much sooner? If you want to do that, there's no better time than right this second to figure out what *one day* will look like.

IS IT A JOB OR A DREAM?

We all do the math and do it more often the older we get. I have to work at this job for X number of years and save Y amount of money so I can retire at Z age. It's the algebra that's been drilled into us since the day we entered the workforce. And frankly, it can be a little depressing to reduce your future to a bunch of numbers on a spreadsheet.

If you can learn to expand your idea of where that equation comes from, you can think outside of the nine-to-five definition. You don't have to have a job, per se. You don't even have to have a career. Instead, you can have a *vision*.

I've never told my kids they need to go to college so that they can get a good job. The word "job" has never come out of my mouth because I don't believe everyone has to have a job. Jobs are a box. You become a timecard, clocking in and out when you're at a job. For many of us, that can be the epitome of a prison sentence.

There was a commercial that aired during the Superbowl in 1999 for Monster.com. The ad is in black and white and features kids finishing the phrase, "When I grow up…" One kid says, "I want to file all day." Another says, "I want to climb my way to middle management," and others say, "be underappreciated, be paid less for the same job."

I remember watching that commercial and thinking, "I am *not* going to be one of those kids." That was the whole point of the commercial—to get people thinking about how the job they have today isn't necessarily the one they dreamed of as a kid.

Now, if your job is something you really love to do, like teaching or obstetrics, that's great. Derek Jeter loved every day he played shortstop for the New York Yankees. If you're going to have a job, it should be one that you really, really want. Nobody wants to be a cog in a cerebral assembly machine, which is something so many jobs are right now.

But what if you could have *more* than a job? What if you could have the dream of doing exactly what you want when you want? You also don't have to stop working or doing what you love in order to play a good game of Chess or Checkers.

There are no rules saying a daycare teacher can't also own the center where she works. Or that an obstetrician can't own his own practice or clinic. Or that a mechanic can't own the shop where she's fixing cars every day. If that teacher, doctor, or mechanic is passionate about living a life that allows them the flexibility to go to the kids' sports games or take a nice vacation a few times a year, then running a business might be the best answer. We'll go more into owning businesses later in this book and talk about the different advantages of thinking about businesses in another way beyond profit and loss statements.

> When you work a job, you are building someone else's dream. Why not build your own?

It's so easy to get stuck in that X-Y-Z equation for retirement. By the time you get to your thirties and forties, you're stuck on the hamster wheel. You have a mortgage, kids, responsibilities, and bills—lots and lots of bills. You're so stuck in paycheck-to-paycheck living that you don't see a way to get off the treadmill to start your own business or change careers. All you see for the next thirty years is more of the same.

To me, there are only two types of "good jobs" to have:

1. The kind that pays you *a lot* of money so that you have a surplus of income, which you can then use to buy assets, such as real estate and/or businesses, that can replace your active income or recurring income with passive income.

2. A job that doesn't pay really well but that gives you enough education to start your own business in that

same field. In my opinion, the best thing you can learn as the manager of Starbucks is how to run a great coffee shop so you can then start your own down the street.

Not very many of us work jobs that pay a ton of money. Most of us work jobs that pay enough to keep up with our bills. Those kinds of jobs remind me of the black and white movies from the thirties and forties where people are working an assembly line, doing the same thing over and over and over again. Walk into any modern office building and you'll see a line of cubicles filled with people doing the same thing over and over and over again. We have replaced the physical assembly line with a cerebral one.

If you hate being an employee, then learn your industry well enough to start your own company, like a coffee shop in the example above. Yes, you might end up competing with your former employer—even if it's on a much smaller scale—but you will have the freedom and opportunity to make what you want. The hours you put in fuel *your* dream, not someone else's. You are in control of your own wealth potential, which sounds a lot better than being stuck on a hamster wheel.

That's a Chess move, because it delivers the very thing most people really want: time and freedom. And here's the thing— you can choose whether you play Chess or Checkers. You can choose far more of the outcome of that game than you realize, which is what the next few chapters will show you.

I think society has made it socially unacceptable to be wealthy. It becomes this bad word, as if you are an overlord with a fiefdom of serfs. It's not a bad word. It's totally okay to want to advance your lifestyle and to live that lifestyle in your retirement. Money, as I said earlier, gives you choices. You can choose not to buy that yacht that the Joneses bought and use that money on a family trip to Europe or to help out a neighbor who has fallen on hard times. Whatever lifestyle you dream of having, that's the one you should fund.

TAXES CAN BE YOUR FRIEND

The biggest retirement misconceptions center around taxes (we are going to get more in depth about taxes later in this book). Most people see taxes as the enemy. All they want to do is avoid them, so they make decisions that can actually end up *costing* them more in the end. Nobody wants to lose money, especially money they worked very hard to earn, so this is where knowing how the math works helps you out.

Let's take the good old 401k, for instance. These retirement vehicles came out in the 70s, around the time most companies stopped handing out pensions. The idea that your retirement could be self-funded and augmented by your employer's contributions seemed fabulous. The premise was you would put in pre-tax money (thereby avoiding the taxes on that portion of your income) and then start drawing from it when you're retired, and theoretically in a lower tax bracket.

Wait—lower tax bracket? Who wants to make *less* money when they're retired and can finally enjoy their money? I know I don't want to be in a lower tax bracket, at least from that standpoint. I want to have the same, or better, lifestyle when I get older. Not to mention, when you are retired, most of your tax deductions (like mortgage interest and kids) are gone, so your tax bracket may not change as much as you think (and may even go up), unless you drastically reduce your taxable income. That's like saying, *Hey, if I'm really broke in retirement, I'll save on taxes and that 401k will go a lot further.*

> In my opinion, that's failure mentality. You are banking on making less money.

I'm not saying that 401ks are a bad idea. I'm definitely not advising you to stop contributing to your 401k. These plans, along with IRA and 403b plans, are considered "qualified money," meaning they are comprised of money that hasn't been taxed yet, which is great and can give you some income when you are retired. However, they were never meant to be the sole vehicle to fund your retirement; and yet, for a lot of us, they are. Lots of people are using their 401k plan as their one and only nest egg. Most people aren't putting anywhere near enough money into their 401k plan (remember those stats I quoted in Chapter One?), so that single nest egg isn't going to go far.

Let's say you have a million dollars in your 401k. Sounds good, right? Using the 4% pulldown rule, which says you draw out only 4% of your 401k each year you are retired, you'll be living on $40,000 a year. Even if your house and car are paid off, $40,000 isn't going to go far. A single medical emergency could wipe you out. The average hospital stay will cost you about $11,000, even with Medicare.[8] Then there are copays on your medications, physical therapy, and lifestyle accommodations. Putting a new roof on the house—$20,000 easily. Buying a new car—$50,000 before you even walk off the lot. We haven't even added in groceries, electricity, or the gas for that new car. That $40,000 will go very, very quickly.

When I was growing up, people talked about retiring to Florida. Maybe buying a little home in a trailer park or one of the villas in The Villages and living out their lives in warm, sunny weather. Ever since the real estate boom in Florida, the prices for even the smallest house are astronomical. The HOA fees for a community like The Villages are high, and if you're living on $40,000 a year, you won't have much left over to go out to dinner or play a round of golf.

Don't you want more from your retirement and life?

Do you think the investment companies (like mutual fund companies) are waiting thirty years to start using the money you're contributing to your 401k? No. Those investment companies are using that cash flow *right now* to invest in

---

8 https://www.ncbi.nlm.nih.gov/books/NBK91989/

other things, and they are making Chess moves to allow their businesses and bank accounts to grow exponentially. That's what makes them successful, and that success helps your investments grow. However, if you want to retire like them, you have to think like them instead of sitting on the sidelines and watching your 401k grow for thirty years. We're going to get into more specifics on how to do that in later chapters.

Don't count on Social Security being there to add to your income. In fact, if you're forty or younger, you should pretend Social Security doesn't even exist and don't factor that money in your retirement plans. That way, you're fine if it's not there. If it is, great, a little extra money every month. That's the key point with Social Security—it's not a lot of money. It's a little bit of money. No one is getting rich off their Social Security payments each month.

In fact, we all know people who are subsisting almost entirely on Social Security, which can be very, *very* tough because Social Security maxes out for everyone at around $4,000[9] a month (assuming you made enough during your working years to qualify for the max). I don't think many of the people who don't have other retirement income are necessarily happy living on that small amount from Social Security. If you asked them, I bet a lot of them would say they wish they had planned ahead better and invested more and/or better.

---

9 https://www.investopedia.com/ask/answers/102814/what-maximum-i-can-receive-my-social-security-retirement-benefit.asp

Your mindset is such a big part of this, which is why I encouraged you to take a minute to dream about the lifestyle you want. Playing a strategic game of Checkers or Chess starts with seeing and believing an abundant life can be yours, rather than spending your days worrying about what's in your bank account and how far that will stretch.

On the opposite side of that, someone with a scarcity mindset might add up all the dollars and cents from their 401k plan and Social Security, do the math, and then try to figure out where they can cut back to make this work. I'm trying to get you out of that scarcity mindset so that you are coming at your retirement from a strategic place. Then, you can really live that retirement you dreamed about a few pages ago.

THE CHESS AND CHECKERS RETIREMENT

The last thing anyone wants to do is run out of money during retirement and be penniless for the rest of their lives. So how are you going to accumulate the wealth that keeps you from worrying about money during those golden years? There is one way that I know that works—by learning to play Chess or Checkers really, really well before you hit retirement. You think ahead, assess what your dreams will cost, and make a plan that gets you there.

> Don't rely on one nest egg to fund everything you want and need.

Let's get into some specifics so that you have some concrete actions you can take if you want to play a good Checkers game. First, if you're getting closer to retirement, get all of your debt paid down or paid off so that you can be in a position to save a lot of money—money that you can use to build your wealth.

Next, figure out how much income you will need in retirement to actually *live*. I'm not talking about how much it could cost to pay your bills. No one wants to pay their bills and sit in their house, staring at the walls and waiting for death to come knocking. You want to go places, do things, have things? How much money will you need to sustain that lifestyle?

Whatever that number is, it's not likely going to be high enough because there's always a good chance the markets will drop, inflation will rise, or the economy will have a downturn, and you want to be prepared for that. You also have to prepare for things like long-term care and medical bills, as well as the amount of money you want to leave to your children. If this is you, it's really good to work with a Checkers financial advisor because they can create a plan for you to follow.

Be realistic about what lifestyle you want and get into the mindset of living that lifestyle right now (that does not mean you should go out and buy a yacht or book a trip to Monaco. You simply want to start thinking like the person living that life would think). This way, you'll go into your Checkers game with the right strategies. Some people want to leave a legacy for their kids (some don't, which is fine as long as you realize your kid will probably end up working for a Chess player later on). Some people want to build a huge corporation; some people want to spend it all before they die. Whatever that answer is or where you fit in those categories, you should know those answers now (and know you might change your mind).

People who play Chess are often thinking about how they will get to checkmate before they move the first pawn, making adjustments along the way to strategize their game. It's the same with financial Chess players. They are looking far into the future and thinking about building generational wealth. They want to build income streams that will last long after they are gone. They don't see retirement as the end game and don't even think about the day after they turn sixty-five. They don't want to retire any more than baseball players want to hang up their gloves. They want to keep building, growing, and moving into new areas. They're always thinking, *What can I do today to get me to the point where I have more time to do what I want? How can I build this faster so I have choices and freedom?*

Checkers players put their money into qualified accounts, pay off their houses, purchase the insurance they need for long-term care and life, and have a plan for what they will do with the rest of their lives.

> ## The whole investment game plan shouldn't be getting just a gold watch and a retirement party.

It should be: *How can I become financially free a lot quicker? How can I compound my lifestyle?*

As a wealth advisor, that's how I want to be judged by my clients. Did I help them compound their lifestyle this year? For instance, if I have a client who took two vacations last year. When they came to me, they said they wanted to vacation more, not less. So we made financial moves that allowed them to afford to take four this year, or choose to make their two vacations much longer stays in dream destinations. When my clients live a better life this year than last, then I have been successful (and so have they).

To me, whether you are playing Chess or Checkers, the important thing is to have a *game plan.* I can't emphasize this enough—you need to have a game plan if you're going to play the game, and most of all, play it well.

"Stay flexible. Be ready to transform advantages from one type to another."

—John Nunn

CHAPTER THREE

TAXES CAN BE YOUR FRIEND

I bet you read the title of this chapter and thought, *that's impossible.* No one likes taxes, right? How can they be a friend?

Wrong. Taxes can, indeed, work for your benefit—and the government's. When that happens, your tax burden can be greatly reduced because the government really, *really* likes it when people do things that benefit it in the long run. The key is in understanding how the government thinks about money.

Taxes get a bad rap because no one likes *paying* taxes. We know we have to do it if we want roads paved and bridges built. Every April 15th, those taxes become a dreaded, necessary event.

Taxes themselves aren't bad. They're simply a vehicle for the government to create income to run itself, pay the defense budget, and build infrastructure. Most of us don't have anything against the *concept* of taxes because we know that they fund our roads and schools—until that money comes out of our paychecks or bank accounts. Then taxes can get very annoying, very fast. Chess players, however, know how to make taxes their friend—in other words, how to make the tax code work for them in legal ways.

> The government, AKA Uncle Sam, has set up many, many ways for you to NOT have to pay taxes because you not paying taxes actually benefits the government.

If you've never thought about it that way, I promise this chapter will change how you look at the tax codes. First, let's talk about the two kinds of taxes: progressive and regressive.

PROGRESSIVE TAX (THE TRICK-OR-TREATING ANALOGY)

A progressive tax is a type of taxation system that levies a higher percentage of income from high-income earners compared to those with lower income. In other words, the more you earn, the higher your tax rate (because you can afford to pay more). It's calculated in what's called tax brackets. But that's not really a fun way to explain the difference between these two kinds of taxes, so let me use my trick-or-treat analogy.

Imagine you lived in a neighborhood with progressive Halloween taxes. The more candy you receive while trick-or-treating, the higher the percentage you have to give back to the community candy bowl. In this scenario, it's important to note that each individual collected as much as they could.

- If you got a small amount of candy, you might only have to give back a small portion to the community bowl.
- But if you collected a large haul of candy, you would be required to contribute a higher percentage of your total candy to the communal bowl. You would be in the higher candy bracket.

1. **First 1 to 10 pieces**: No tax. These people are at the candy poverty level

2. **11 to 44 pieces (Taxed at 12%):**

    - If you have 44 pieces, the tax on the first 44 pieces would be12% of 44. So 0.12 * 44 = 5.28 pieces (rounded down to 5 pieces)

3. **45 to 95 pieces (Taxed at 22%):**

    - The first 44 pieces are taxed at 12%, which equals 5 pieces paid for tax
    - The next 51 pieces (95 - 44 = 51) are taxed at 22%. 22% of 51 is 0.22 * 51 = 11.22 pieces (rounded down to 11 pieces)

4. **Next 96 to 182 pieces (Taxed at 24%):**

    - The first 44 pieces are taxed at 12%, which equals 5 pieces paid for tax

- The next 51 pieces are taxed at 22%, which equals 11 pieces paid for tax
- The remaining 87 pieces in this range (182 - 95 = 87) are taxed at 24%. 24% of 87 or 0.24 * 87 = 20.88 pieces (rounded down to 20 pieces)

5. **Next 183 to 231 pieces (Taxed at 32%):**

   - The first 44 pieces are taxed at 12%, which equals 5 pieces paid for tax
   - The next 51 pieces are taxed at 22%, which equals 11 pieces paid for tax
   - The next 87 pieces are taxed at 24%, which equals 20 pieces paid for tax
   - The remaining 49 pieces (231 - 182 = 49) are taxed at 32%. 32% of 49 or 0.32 * 49 = 15.68 pieces (rounded down to 15 pieces)

If you add up the taxes from each range: 5 (12%) + 11 (22%) + 20 (24%) + 15 (32%) = 51 pieces. You have paid 51 pieces of your 250 pieces of candy collected toward the communal candy bowl, based on the progressive tax rates. This would be roughly 20.4% of your candy income.

REGRESSIVE CANDY TAX ANALOGY

Now, consider two individuals:

Person A:

- Collected 20 candies.

- 15% of 20 candies or 0.15 * 20 = 3 candies contributed to the communal bowl.

Person B:

- Collected 200 candies.
- 15% of 200 candies or 0.15 * 200 = 30 candies contributed to the communal bowl.

IMPACT ON DIFFERENT INCOME LEVELS

Another example of a regressive tax are sales taxes. Consider two individuals purchasing the same car priced at $50,000, but they have different annual incomes. The sales tax on the car is a flat 9%, which works out to approximately $4,500. For someone making $100,000, that's 4.5% of their income for that year, but for someone making a million dollars, that sales tax bill is only 0.45% of their income.

The main difference between progressive and regressive taxes is how they affect people with different income levels. A progressive tax has a greater impact on higher-income individuals, while a regressive tax has a greater impact on lower-income individuals.

THE DADDY TAX

There was a gas station next to the daycare my kids attended and every time I picked them up, they'd ask for me to take them there to pick out some candy. Once in a while, I'd indulge them, but also used it as a lesson to explain how taxes work.

After I paid for their chosen candy bars, I broke off a small piece of the candy to eat and called it the "Daddy Tax" (which, incidentally, worked out well for me because then I didn't end up eating an entire candy bar). If they complained, I explained to them that it was in their best interests to buy a candy bar that I didn't like, because then I wouldn't want a piece of it, and thus, I wouldn't take a Daddy Tax.

My daughter understood that concept very quickly. She would walk around the gas station, pick up a candy bar and ask me if I liked it. If I said yes, she'd put that candy bar back and move on to the next one. Eventually she realized that I don't like Almond Joys (chocolate and coconut do not go together for me; coconut and rum do, but my daughter's not buying those kinds of candy bars) but she loves them. She typically chose an Almond Joy when we were in the store so she got to eat the entire candy bar herself. If she had opted for a Snickers or a Mars Bar, I would have taken a Daddy Tax bite, which was not what she wanted. Smart kid wanted the entire candy bar.

It's the exact *opposite* for the government. What the government likes, the citizen gets to keep a higher percentage of, which means, if you do what the government wants you to do, you get to keep a higher percentage of your money.

I bet you want to keep the *entire* candy bar of your money, or at the very least, a lot more of it than you are already keeping. Am I right?

ONE REASON WHY THE WEALTHY DON'T PAY A LOT OF TAXES

Before I talk about specifics, let's talk about how the top Chess players, AKA the wealthy, are managing to legally avoid paying taxes. They know there are basically three ways to make money (and this is a very general example):

1. *Earned Income*—this is the money you earn at your job, and it's usually taxed heavily.

2. *Portfolio Income*—these are the capital gains you earn on the sale of anything in your portfolio, like capital gains from stocks and bonds or dividend income earned from bonds and other such securities. Portfolio income is also likely not subject to Social Security and/or Medicare taxes.

3. *Passive Income*—this is the dream, the money that flows into your bank account without you having to "materially participate" in the act of earning it. Passive income can be offset by passive losses, like depreciation. There are plenty of incentives set in place by the IRS for real estate investments, which we'll get to in a minute.

Passive Income—this is the dream, the money that flows into your bank account without you having to "materially participate" in the act of earning it. Passive income can be offset by passive losses, like depreciation. There are plenty of incentives set in place by the IRS for real estate investments, which we'll get to in a minute.

Chess players are smart, but are not necessarily geniuses. They understand how taxes work (or hire people who do), and they take advantage of the options that allow them to avoid paying taxes. Notice I said avoid? Tax avoidance is good and legal, and we'll get into why in a second. Now, if you're playing Checkers, you don't have a lot of options to offset your tax burden. This is where Chess players work the game to their advantage.

A lot of people get upset that there are so many "loopholes" available to the wealthy that allow them to avoid paying taxes. Think of them like coupons. A store sends you a coupon for 20% off a big-ticket item. You go in, buy the item, save your 20%, and the cashier thanks you for patronizing the store.

The customer behind you in line is buying the same item but doesn't have a coupon. They start ranting and raving, wanting to know why you got the item so much cheaper. The answer is simple: you took the time to read about the coupon and use it. Not everyone does that, and so they can't be mad that they didn't get the discount. The government is also sending coupons in a way, but not everyone opens the envelope, or uses them. If you don't use the coupon, you're going to be unhappy come tax time.

You just have to make sure you have the right coupon at the right time. For instance: if you make money from things like renting out a property, the government gives you incentives like depreciation (which I'll explain in a second).

In this context, depreciation is good. Depreciation on your car sucks, but depreciation in real estate is good because it offsets the income, and can sometimes negate it altogether.

Plus, if you happen to hit a bump in the road and lose money on investments or rental properties, you can use those losses to lower how much the government takes from your wins in that same category. It's a way of essentially balancing the scales. To me, these aren't loopholes, they're just rules and they're for everyone. If you understand the rules, you can benefit from them, too.

I get asked all the time, "What book should I read about investments?" My answer? "Before you read a book on investments, you should read a book on taxes, like *Tax-Free Wealth* by Tom Wheelwright CPA."

Just to be 100% clear: *Tax avoidance is good and legal. Tax evasion is bad and illegal.* The difference between the two is simple: I made this money, and the rules set in place by the government say that what I chose to do with that money has a tax benefit (on some or all of the money), therefore I get to avoid paying taxes vs. I don't want to pay taxes so I'm going to evade and not report them, and ultimately…go to prison. The first option is definitely the best one.

If you have the right mindset and are willing to put in a little work to understand the rules and how you can benefit from them, you can find and take advantage of these options. Start by looking at the concept of government, taxes, and investments in a different way, and begin to see the strategies that will elevate your Chess game. There is much more to playing the game than simply paying Uncle Sam every April.

What's the definition of insanity? If you ask a hundred people, they'll probably say: Doing the same thing over and over again and expecting a different result. Webster's definition of insanity doesn't have any of those words.

> Insanity: unsoundness of mind or lack of the ability to understand that prevents someone from having the mental capacity required by law to enter into a particular relationship, status, or transaction or that releases someone from criminal or civil responsibility.[10]

---

10 https://www.merriam-webster.com/dictionary/insanity

We have been programmed to believe the definition of insanity is one thing when in fact, it's another. It's the same with funding your future. There is more than one way to get there, and tax avoidance is part of taking the highway instead of the meandering backroads.

TAX CODES ARE A GUIDELINE ON HOW NOT TO PAY TAXES

Back when I was a rookie police officer, I was sitting in the cafeteria of the courthouse when a well-respected judge, Judge Simmons, walked up to my table. "I hear you're a baseball guy," he said.

"Yes, I played in college and now I coach at West Springfield High School," I told him, wondering why this judge was asking me about sports.

He said, "Okay, when you're in my courtroom, I want you to always pitch the ball right down the middle. When you do that, it's a strike every time. If you start messing with those corners, some judges will call it a ball, others will call it a strike, and you will feel a lot of stress because you won't know which it will be. But if you throw the ball right down the middle, you know you're always doing the right thing."

The judge was right. By playing by the rules and not trying to skirt them or bend them, you will be far more successful. I used that saying in police work and now in my finance work when I explain to people that there are many legal ways to do something, and when you know and use those ways, you're going to be fine. You don't have to mess with the corners. When it comes to taxes, know the rules, and pitch the ball right down the middle, you'll throw a strike every time. If you start fudging the numbers and trying to squeeze a square peg in a round hole, it's going to end badly for you.

One of those rules is pretty clear and is right there in the Internal Revenue Code book (which in 2023, was a huge 1,776 pages long): "All gross income is taxable, from whatever source derived."

What that means is that if you earn money at your job, realized (had earned) income on your investments, or if you pick up a dollar off the street, you owe taxes on that income. Legally, you are supposed to claim every dollar you receive as income and pay a tax on that income. We all know that when we file our taxes every April and for some of us, that payment is painful because we weren't prepared for it. Or we realize we overpaid taxes all year out of our paychecks, which means we just gave the government an interest-free loan. Either way, that's not the best strategy.

However, there are legal ways to not pay some, most, or all of your taxes and to use that money to build your wealth. Essentially, if you do things that the government likes and that ultimately benefit the U.S. government and economy, you get to keep more of your money.

WHY THE GOVERNMENT INCENTIVIZES YOU TO OWN A BUSINESS

Businesses of all sizes are given many tax breaks for several reasons. One huge reason is simple: Business owners who are making money will create jobs. Those W-2 employees pay taxes, and again, bring revenue into the government. Giving a business owner a break can result in multiple employees paying taxes, which will possibly offset any loss the government might have on taxes the owner might have paid.

WHY THE GOVERNMENT WANTS YOU TO OWN MULTIPLE PIECES OF REAL ESTATE

Real estate investors who buy properties to rent create housing and competitive, natural rent control. When there are more available rental properties for people to choose from, the government doesn't have to get involved in setting rent control limits or policies. More people living in a particular area brings in more income for that area, creating more infrastructure.

In the tax code, there is a status known as "Real Estate Professional" or REP status. This means that real estate investing is your day-to-day, primary focus. If you are able to have REP status, the depreciation on the properties is now considered active, not passive, because you are "materially participating" in the real estate investing. This depreciation allows the offset of what would otherwise be passive income and allows real estate investors to pay very little to no taxes. The godfather of this rule (like him or hate him), is Donald Trump, and is the biggest reason he does not have to pay a lot of taxes, if any. This is one of the biggest tax weapons real estate investors use.

Also, if your spouse is the real estate professional (and you file jointly), it is possible that the depreciation loss on the properties can offset active income from the other spouse. Being a realtor or having a real estate license does not automatically grant you REP status. Speak to a tax professional if you feel like you may qualify for this.

WHY THE GOVERNMENT DOESN'T TAX MUNICIPAL BOND INCOME

At certain levels (especially if you invest in municipal bonds in the state where you reside), the interest on municipal bonds is generally tax-free. This is one of the very few components of your market-based portfolio income that may not increase your tax bill. Why would the government want to incentivize these investments? Because purchasing that municipal bond helps that particular location to improve its infrastructure or some other benefit, which encourages more people to move there, which equates to more property taxes for that area (the fancy-schmancy word for that is *ad valorem* taxes).

Because the risk is very low, a lot of times the interest on municipal bonds isn't very high since the municipality has the power to increase taxes to pay back the bonds. Overall, it is a mutually-beneficial relationship where Chess players and the government or municipality both win from the investments. Simply put, governments borrow money (go into debt) from Chess players (wealthy people) to build schools, roads, bridges, etc. You know what that means? The municipalities and government are also playing Chess.

WHY THE GOVERNMENT WANTS YOU TO HAVE KIDS

Have you ever stopped to think about why the government gives you a tax break on dependents? This is a smaller concept than the others I just mentioned, but the overall reasons are basically the same. It's not because they feel sorry for parents. It's because you having kids does something very beneficial to the government: It creates more taxpayers.

You having children is essentially increasing the tax base which, in the end, is a good thing for the government because it gives them more people to tax, which equals more tax revenue. They encourage people to have kids by giving them a break on their income taxes because the government knows those kids will grow up and a lot of them will be W-2 earners who will be taxed heavily and bring revenue into the government coffers.

WHY THE GOVERNMENT WANTS YOU TO INVEST IN OIL DRILLING

Investing in oil and gas production has a number of tax benefits (other sources of energy do, too, but the biggest benefits are found in oil and gas). There are investment options such as direct participation programs that allow a group of accredited investors (meaning, people with significant wealth or income) to pool their money and fund drilling operations.

The government offers numerous tax breaks for intangible drilling costs (wages, insurance premiums, and other costs on things that cannot be salvaged) and depletion allowances (the oil eventually runs out) because energy is what makes the world go around, and the more the U.S. government can produce, the less it needs to rely on other countries.

To participate in this kind of thing, you must have a lot of money. This isn't investing in stock for Exxon, or other oil and gas companies. This is a large-scale type of investment that is typically just for **accredited** investors (people who meet a certain wealth and income threshold). Hopefully, in the future, these great tax benefits will apply to renewable sources of energy. In my opinion, if the tax breaks applied to oil and gas drilling are also applied to renewable energy sources, companies will more quickly adopt and implement these options because there is an incentive for them to do so.

> In order to play Chess, real estate has to be on your board. It's likely going to be part of your financial strategy. It's hard to play Chess without owning real estate.

Knowing these strategies helps you make better decisions that can possibly lower your tax burden. When you don't spend your money on these types of things that the government likes, Uncle Sam is going to take his bite (or an even larger bite), just like I do with the candy bars my kids buy. Yes, we live in a free country. And yes, we have free will to decide what we want to do. The government still has rules that basically say, "If you choose not to put your money in these kinds of investments, we will tax you because we still need to use tax money to run the government."

There aren't a lot of other ways to significantly lower your taxes, especially if you have a modest or average income. Most people can't afford to invest in oil and gas production; many people are done having kids; not everyone is interested in owning a business. It is, however, something to know about and aspire to as an option for your investing. For almost all of us, real estate is one option that is accessible to pretty much everyone with some available investment income.

UNDERSTANDING THE TAX BREAKS IN REAL ESTATE

Before you start investing, you should understand how taxes and real estate work. You don't have to become a certified public accountant or an enrolled agent, but you may want to work with one, and read books or take a class so that you have a working knowledge. Otherwise, you might make decisions that could harm you come tax season.

Real estate depreciation, for instance, is different from the kind of depreciation that happens when you drive a new car off the lot. Property depreciation and costs for repairs can be used to offset the income that the property generated.

We've established that the government wants you to buy and invest in real estate, so they have made it possible to retain some or all of the capital gains you receive. For instance, when you sell an investment property, they incentivize you to buy more real estate with the money or, more likely, trade up.

By buying property with a higher value, another that is valued the same, or buying multiple properties with the profits you made on selling the first piece, you can defer the taxes on those capital gains, something that is called a 1031 Exchange. Think of it like trading four little green houses in Monopoly for one red hotel.

If you keep doing this until you die, the government basically dismisses all the taxes you would have paid when you were alive. Your heirs will get what's called a "step-up in basis" and not owe taxes on the capital gains if they sell the property for the same value it holds on the date of your death.

For example, let's say I bought a rental property for $1 million that is worth $2 million the day I die. If I sold it the day *before* I died, I'd pay capital gains tax on the profit I made. However, if the property was still in my estate when I died and my kids inherit it—and promptly sell it for what it's worth ($2 million)—they won't owe any taxes because they got a step-up in basis. This is a key to generational wealth building. This is also true for other types of investments, which we'll get into a little later in this book.

The 1031 Exchange works so well for real estate because the capital gains on the first property are tax-deferred for you while you're alive, and then, if you die still owning the little red hotel, your heirs get that step-up in basis and may not pay any taxes when they sell that piece of property (especially if it is at the same fair market value as it was the day of your death). Other things go into this concept, but those are outside the scope of this book. I'm just giving you a general explanation.

Then, let's say the kids don't sell it and it goes up in value. Your heirs would only pay the capital gains tax on the difference in market value between the day of your death and what they sell it for. The key here, however, is to not sell the property, but rather to use it as collateral…a strategy we discuss in the next part of this book.

Real estate is a swap-until-you-drop kind of game.

Be careful, however, because there are a lot of rules to selling real estate if you want to avoid paying capital gains taxes. You should definitely work with someone who knows how to effectively conduct a 1031 Exchange. Your local salt-of-the-earth realtor may not be that person. You need a team of professionals who understand those rules and can guide you in making the right decisions.

You also should work with a tax professional because there are a lot of rules to these particular Chess strategies and, if you want to succeed, you need to partner with people who know those rules *inside and out*. You don't want to mess something up and inadvertently create a huge tax liability you didn't expect. There are fairly strict rules to meeting some of these tax statutes, so make sure you find professionals who are familiar with them.

There is no one-size-fits-all answer, which is why I encourage you to research the options and know your specific goals before you start investing in anything. Know that the big guys—a lot of those corporations you give your money to, especially financial institutions—are investing in these things to grow their corporate income and avoid taxes. And if they're doing it, there's no reason you can't, too. You're just probably going to do it on a much smaller scale.

> It's all about understanding the rules of Chess and then playing with a strategy that brings you closer to living your dream life.

"I feel sorry for players who are always lying awake at night, brooding over their games."

—Magnus Carlson

CHAPTER FOUR

STOP TRYING TO OUTSMART THE MARKET

One of the most common questions I hear as a wealth advisor is: Can the market create wealth? The answer is: Kind of.

The main goal of many of the people investing in the stock market is capital appreciation (which is, essentially, buy low, sell high). You can certainly make money doing that, but becoming wealthy is much less of a sure thing.

We just had one of the longest running bull markets in US history. Who do you know that got wealthy from that? And I mean wealthy in the context of being able to quit their job and buy a house on an island, or whatever your definition of wealthy is. I'll give you a minute to think about it. Anyone in your immediate circle? Outside your immediate circle? Friends of your outer immediate circle?

Chances are, you don't know anyone who got wealthy during that bull market (or the one before, or the one before that). Does that mean nobody got wealthy from the bull market run? Not at all. It just means the chances of it happening *to you* are small. The market is capable of delivering those kinds of large returns, but to get those you're going to have to take large investing risks and that may not be good for your situation. If you're investing responsibly, the truth is you're probably not going to be able to achieve enough of a return on the stock market to leave your 9 to 5.

The fact is, there aren't a lot of truly wealthy people in the world.[11] This graph[12] indicates how stark the difference is between the super-wealthy and most people. The very richest (meaning people with more than $38 million dollars) make up just 0.1% of the population, which is only about 131,000 people total.

11 https://www.statista.com/statistics/203961/wealth-distribution-for-the-us/

12 https://www.visualcapitalist.com/wealth-distribution-in-america/#google_vignette

CAN YOU BEAT THE MARKET?

Your goal should never be to "beat the market" because, to do that, you have to outsmart a whole lot of people. There are some very talented people and a lot of computer algorithms trying to do the same thing; and if you are smarter than a computer algorithm, then be my guest. Most of us, frankly, aren't. My job as a wealth advisor is not to beat the market; it's to help you build your wealth.

There's an old saying that it's not timing the market, it's time *in* the market that brings you the most success. I have found this to be true. If you can afford to let your money sit for ten years or more, and you continue to see a nice, upward pattern, then you should make money off your investment.

The question is: *How much time do you have on this earth, and how much money did you start with?*

In my opinion, compound interest is one of the most oversold concepts in investing today, especially because the math is irrefutable. Let's say you have a nice, healthy 7% rate of return on the stocks you bought. On average, your money should double every ten years. That sounds great, right?

But how many sets of ten years do you have? What if you start investing that money when you're fifty or sixty, or even seventy? Do you have that much time to sit around and wait for it to double? And wait for it to double again? And again?

And what kind of money are you putting into the market? If you invest $100 at age twenty (and assuming you don't add any more money to that account), it'll double by the time you're thirty to $200. Then $400 by the time you're forty, $800 at fifty, and a whopping $1600 by the age of sixty. Add inflation and other obstacles and you will see how hard it is to actually save the kind of money you need for retirement.

Let's change those numbers and say you invested $10 million dollars. When that doubles to $20 million, that's a nice increase. If you have $10 million dollars to start with, you obviously have more resources than the general population, which means you have the means to create the income you need to live a very comfortable life.

Here's the secret, though: The people who have $10 million to invest aren't sitting around and watching their grass grow. They are actively building their wealth.

Remember that Temu commercial from the Super Bowl in 2024? It showed people buying lots of fancy stuff, saying they could "shop like a billionaire" on Temu because the prices are so low. I laughed when I saw it because the average costs for products on Temu are very, very low (because they are knockoffs of Gucci, et.al., not the real thing) and when you put those costs against the average American income, it can definitely *feel* like shopping billionaire-style. It's the relationship between your income and the cost of their goods that gives you that perception of "shopping like a billionaire." But it's a mirage; it's not the same as actually having the income to buy perhaps higher quality goods and not worry about paying the mortgage.

The simple truth is that humans just don't live long enough to see the kinds of returns they'd like, especially if they're not starting out with a lot of money to begin with. Maybe if you lived nine hundred years like Yoda did, compound interest alone could drastically change your lifestyle. By your four hundredth year, you'd be rolling in dough.

THE GAMBLER'S MENTALITY

The people who live with a gambler's mentality think they'll strike it rich if they just pick the right stock. That's not likely to happen, especially given the way the majority of people invest. Most of us don't play the stock market like we play roulette, putting all of our money on one stock that we hope will turn into the next Amazon because the truth is, people don't know who the next Amazon will be. If we did, we'd all be rich. And let's face it; it's not the responsible thing to put your life savings into one startup company.

People generally invest in the market through their retirement and brokerage accounts, such as 401ks, IRAs or 403bs, etc. When they do, they've very likely made choices based on their risk tolerance. But even if you opt for a high-risk investment strategy, it's difficult to be able to create enough wealth through the stock market to live the kind of life people dream of having. The average man in his forties and fifties only has a couple hundred thousand in his 401k. It's almost impossible to become a multi-millionaire before retirement if you are starting with less than a quarter million dollars.

I have a running joke at seminars that goes something like this: "If you go up to someone at the boat show who owns a $25 million yacht and ask them how they afforded it, they aren't likely to respond with, 'I killed it with my IRA.'" I get a good chuckle out of that comment because an IRA (or 401k or other retirement investment product) is unlikely to be your path to a $25 million yacht.

People laugh at my joke because they know, deep down in their souls, that playing a Checkers game is unlikely to make them wealthy. You can retire, but it's far-fetched to think you'll spend that retirement sitting on a $25 million yacht. Your kids likely won't be able to do that, either. In fact, no one in your family will probably be able to do that unless you switch to playing Chess and teach those strategies to the next generation.

Investing in market-based assets to build wealth is not an impossible thing because some people can do very well in the market. It's simply oversold as a great way to fund a retirement and lifestyle. Market-based assets shouldn't be your sole strategy. They need to be part of a bigger picture. Retirement plans could be another cog in the wheel of your plan—just not the whole wheel.

Chess players know they can leverage their investments to fund other investments and create income strategies. Chess players see beyond the bi-weekly contributions to what they can do with that money. Chess players think beyond the standard options and model the wealthy.

You might think that you can become wealthy if you only invest in the S&P 500 index (which is the list of the top 500 companies, according to Standard & Poor) because the S&P 500 is often used as a gauge for the health of the overall stock market. The S&P 500 isn't the entire stock market; think of it more like taking the stock market's temperature at any given time.

Those index funds can be a nice, solid investment option, especially if you aren't interested in diving deeper into finances or don't want to pay someone to help you invest. However, the idea that *everyone* should just invest in the S&P 500 is nuts.

Just extrapolate this for a second—if everyone put all their money into a total of around five hundred companies, all the other companies' stocks would be worth zero. By extension, the auto manufactures could be in the S&P, but the suppliers would not be since the suppliers are unlikely to be included in the top 500 companies. The vendors that Ford and Chevy rely on to make the tires for their cars or the metal for the frames would eventually have financial problems. That could create a terrible domino effect.

Also, if everybody abided by the "only invest in the S&P 500" rule, then all new companies would be worthless because they would not be able to sell their Initial Public Offering. No one would buy shares because everyone is solely investing in those other five hundred companies.

Translation: There would be no new publicly traded companies, like Amazon and Google were a couple decades ago. No new Nvidia stock, no new Disney stock, etc. Let me be clear: Investing in the S&P 500 can be good, but that doesn't mean every person on the planet should do it as their sole investment strategy.

THE CHESS MINDSET WITH THE STOCK MARKET

Chess players know the market is just one of many ways to build wealth. The market is a tried-and-true option that, over time, has proven to go up, but can also get hit by massive dips, like in 2008. It's easily accessible, you can start with very little money (which also begs the question, if pretty much anyone can invest in the market nowadays, why aren't more people getting rich from it?). They also know that it's almost impossible to pick that one correct stock and that, if they go into it with a gambler's mindset, they're likely to have a gambler's outcome.

> The goal of any casino is to make money, not to have you win; so, don't play the market like it's a giant casino.

The Chess mindset sees the market as a way to qualify for loans they can then use for other investments or even their own income. Chess players know they can get those kinds of loans because their portfolio shows they have the resources to pay the lender back if they had to.

To clarify, the Chess player doesn't *want* to pay the loan back with his or her own money. They want to pay it back with *someone else's* money. That money would come from the income they made from what they bought with the loan, whether that's a business or a piece of real estate. The market is a tool for them to show, on paper, they have the resources. In other words, I don't want to use my money, I want the banker to go into the vault so I can use some of the bank's money.

The Chess player isn't just building wealth for himself or herself, they are trying to build *generational wealth.* They know (because they read the last chapter) that leaving investments like real estate to their heirs allows their heirs to have a step-up in basis.

Just as I mentioned with real estate, capital gains taxes work similarly with stocks when you die. If Grandpa bought Apple stock in 1980 and held onto it until he died, his heirs wouldn't owe taxes on that stock if they sold it at whatever value it was at the date of his death, because they have a step-up in basis.

Grandpa knows that building his dream lifestyle isn't about selling that stock to cash out—it's about using that portfolio almost like a collateral resource to buy assets that will bring in regular income, likely with tax benefits, from someone else's money (like properties he rents out).

Checkers players are looking at the market-based assets as a means to supplement their income a little; Chess players see the market as a collateral opportunity for loans that will buy assets that bring in income every month.

Here's the irony in all this: The banks are loaning the Checkers' players money (savings deposits) to the Chess players. As we all know, banks don't keep millions of dollars in cash on hand. They use your deposits for investments and loans. So, if you are a Chess player asking for a million-dollar loan to buy a property, the money the bank lends you partially (or entirely) came from deposits Checkers players made.

This isn't wrong; it's how the game is played. I'm not saying don't invest your money in banks. I am saying, if you do and you want to play Chess, then you may want to use a similar strategy as the bank and create income for yourself.

"When you see a good move, look
for a better one."

— Emanuel Lasker

CHAPTER FIVE

WHAT WOULD MASSMUTUAL DO?

When I was a police officer, I had an evidence-based mindset. I wasn't as interested in what you said as I was in how your feet moved, as the old saying goes. Essentially, your actions mattered more than your words. When you watch how the people around you move, especially those who are going in the direction you want to go, you can easily learn what to do to become more like them.

We've been so ingrained with hearing data and information and "must-do" advice, however, that we often don't watch what those same advice-givers are doing. What money moves are they making? Instead of just listening to what they say, you have to look at how they are moving.

The people who play Chess well often disrupt the game; they look for new ways to maximize their positions and gains, meaning they make moves that sometimes go against the typical advice they hear. I want you to always do what you feel comfortable with when it comes to risk, and know what you are giving up if you choose not to make a particular move.

Before you make your next commercial bank deposit, though, I want you to think about what the bank is doing with that money. And why the bank's headquarters is usually a skyscraper in a major metropolitan city.

As you write that check for your insurance policy, stop and think about how that insurance company became so financially healthy. Why do you think flight attendants try to get you to apply for a credit card every single time you're on a plane? Think about it. Continue to ask questions about the companies you use, such as: "Why is this flight attendant trying to get me to apply for this particular card? What other business is this airline invested in that's making it money?"

When you get behind the wheel of your car, I want you to think about what moves that automobile manufacturer made to become so financially strong?

It's likely not just by selling cars (or insurance policies, or mortgages). The major corporate players in the world are doing what you should be doing. They're playing Chess. And they're playing it well.

THE DRAWBACK OF BANKS

These days, a savings account at a bank is pretty much just a glorified mattress to stuff your money into. You're not going to become wealthy by investing your money in products that deliver returns that don't usually keep up with inflation rates. Frankly, that's a guaranteed loss for you.

The banks, however, are not losing money, and they're certainly not keeping all their cash in the savings accounts they sell to customers. They're pretty upfront about what you will earn if you invest with them. Every time I walk into a bank, I see billboards with interest rates, terms, and estimated returns.

Their margins are far greater than yours, however. And they've set up a system that is very likely going to return positive results (unless they make bad loans) because the loans they give out to people like you and me are being funded by people like you and me who make deposits.

In *It's a Wonderful Life,* that Christmas classic with Jimmy Stewart as the intrepid George Bailey, George explains to the panicked customers that the money they are looking for isn't actually in the bank's vault. "You're thinking of this place all wrong, as if I had the money back in a safe," he says. "The money's not here. Your money's in Joe's house...and a hundred others."

The money you borrow isn't inside the bank's safe, nor is the money you deposited and see on your statements. The majority of the bank's money is being invested in mortgages and businesses and other options that pay back the principal with interest,

That becomes a problem when there's a run on the bank, as George's customers found out in that panicked scene early in the movie. Commercial banks are insured by the FDIC up to $250,000, so if there's a run on the bank, you are only insured for to a $250,000 claim.

The Federal Deposit Insurance Corporation (FDIC) is like a safety net. Banks sometimes fail when they take too many risks, like giving loans to people who can't pay them back. But with FDIC insurance, your money is protected even if the bank shuts down. Sometimes, like with the Silicon Valley Bank and Signature Bank, the government will step in to cover more than the usual $250,000 limit.

What if several large banks failed at the same time? It's possible the FDIC wouldn't have enough money to cover the amount insured, or that the government may print enough money to meet those obligations (and thus, probably raises inflation). Remember, they're only insuring $250,000, not the current purchase power of those funds, so if inflation hits…it won't be a good time for anyone.

FDIC insurance also covers different kinds of accounts like checking, savings, and CDs, but it doesn't cover things like stocks or mutual funds. It's important to know that the $250,000 limit applies to each *person*, not each account. So, if you have more than $250,000 in one bank, you might want to spread it out across different accounts between you and your spouse or even to different banks to make sure it's all protected.

There's no stack of cash inside the bank's vaults, either. Banks are required to keep a pretty small percentage of their deposits in cash on hand. The rest of the money is in, as George said, "Joe's house and hundreds of others."

I'm not saying that putting your money in a bank account is a bad idea. Everyone needs operating accounts for the money that comes in as income and goes out as payments. If you've invested in a lot of rental properties, you should have some liquid savings to pay for a new HVAC system or repair the roof after a storm.

But after you meet your own personal threshold for emergency cash, keeping the rest of your money in a commercial bank is probably not the best idea, especially when it could be earning you much higher returns. The banks know this—and so should you.

Wells Fargo, for instance, is one of the top five commercial banks in the country, with nearly $2 trillion in assets and more than 60 million customers. While the bank makes money on lending people money, as most commercial banks do, Wells Fargo also has a strong acquisition strategy to buy smaller banks (and the real estate that comes with the locations). They also have a big wholesale banking division, which focuses on things like equipment and project financing for wholesale customers with at least $5 million in annual revenue.[13] In other words, they are investing in a lot more than just houses. And they're not the only ones. Mutual fund companies (the technical term for these is investment companies), insurance companies…all major industries do similar things.

WHAT ABOUT MUTUAL FUNDS?

There is nothing inherently wrong with mutual funds. They have diversified holdings, so if one individual stock drops, chances are good that another one is climbing. Investing in them can be great, but I want you to think about how the investment company you are using for your investment is becoming wealthy. They are very likely diversifying their holdings into things like real estate and other businesses.

> Just to reiterate what I said earlier: When I talk about diversification, I don't mean stocks, bonds, and mutual funds, because those are all market-based. I mean diversifying between asset classes like market-based assets, real estate, businesses, heck, even cryptocurrency.

---

13 https://www.investopedia.com/articles/markets/093014/how-wells-fargo-became-biggest-bank-america.asp

Mutual funds got really popular in the early 80s. Today, they are everywhere, and nearly everyone's 401k has mutual funds. I have my clients' money invested in some very large and successful investment companies. Some of them also happen to be my biggest competitors in Chess. More than once, one of these very companies (or a company they own/control) that I'm putting mine and my clients' investments in has beat me out on a real estate deal.

That's because those companies are playing Chess, which means sometimes I'm the dog under the table trying to catch whatever they drop on the floor. Where are these companies getting the money to beat out mere mortals, like me and my friends, on real estate deals?

The answer is simple: From me, my clients, and all the other clients of financial advisors who are investing their money in these funds. A lot of financial advisors are still trying to steer their clients clear of these types of investments. They might have good intentions, but it's important to know *why* they are doing that. Maybe the financial advisor doesn't want you having more of your money in assets that he or she can't make money from? As a wealth advisor, I see the board differently. To me, the more wealth *you* build, the better everything will be for all of us, which creates a mutually beneficial relationship.

WHAT ABOUT LIFE INSURANCE?

Before 2020, I used to joke in seminars that the only thing that could take down a life insurance company would be a life-threatening pandemic. Turned out the COVID pandemic was actually very good for the insurance business. It not only didn't bring any of the big life insurance companies down, many of them actually *thrived* during and after the pandemic.

How could that be? Life insurance is about dying, and it doesn't seem like the insurance companies would have a good year during a time when life is deteriorating. It wouldn't have been an unreasonable prediction to expect them to have a down year but still remain a good company in 2020, and continue to do so in 2021, 2022, and so on.

There are two logical explanations for that kind of growth during a global pandemic for a company that insures life when people are rapidly dying, neither of which would be the right answer. First, you might think they didn't pay their claims and kept the money, for some kind of small print pandemic clause or other reason. That's not what happened. The reputable insurance companies paid out the claims as they agreed. Second, you might think that life insurance sales soared during the pandemic because everyone was scared they were going to die, so they rushed out to buy a policy on themselves and everyone in their family they have an insurable interest in, like their kids. Yes, more policies were sold, but not a significant number.

WHAT WOULD MASSMUTUAL DO?

What did go up significantly in 2020 and 2021? Real estate (and the market in 2021 and 2022). People who were working from home decided to move to warmer climates or to their dream location. The real estate market across the country moved at lightning speed and housing prices went through the roof.

And you know who has significant investments in the real estate market? Life insurance companies (as do investment companies, banks, etc.). They have been smart enough to be very well diversified in the type of assets that they own. Even during the pandemic, a lot of these assets were able to maintain cash flow and provide great capital appreciation, especially when it came to residential real estate.

You've probably stayed in a hotel that an insurance company owns. Maybe you rented an apartment in a building owned by an insurance company, or shopped at a mall that an insurance company owns. That's because they invest in a variety of industries and businesses, just like the best Chess players do. Again, this could be indirect ownership.

I'm not going to get into a debate about insurance, and whether you should be buying term or permanent/whole life insurance, because those are topics for another book. I'm just using these companies as an example. I'm also not saying these companies are doing anything wrong. It's the contrary; I'm saying they are doing things right. It's just not what you are likely doing or conditioned to do, and it's not likely what those companies' financial advisor agents are instructing you to do. They are probably not telling you to copy the Chess moves the insurance company is making, but rather encouraging you to invest in the company's products (thereby giving the company more capital to play Chess).

It's all about changing how you look at the everyday choices you make, and seeing how those very companies you are handing your money to are building wealth on the checks you give them.

MassMutual, for example, is an excellent life insurance company and one of those that did very well during the pandemic. Part of the benefit of having a policy with a mutual life insurance company like MassMutual, New York Life, and Northwestern Mutual is that the policies pay dividends. It's not guaranteed, but these companies have paid them through depressions, world wars, and everything else. When a mutual life insurance company makes money, they give some of it back to their policy holders in the form of dividends. In 2021, MassMutual paid out $1.7 billion in dividends to its policy holders.

MassMutual's dividend payouts increased to $1.8 billion in 2022, and $1.9 billion in 2023[14], as the company continued to do better each year. MassMutual is just one example. Let's look at two other big players and see how they did during those years.

---

14 https://www.massmutual.com/about-us/news-and-press-releases/
   press-releases/2022/11/record-policyowner-dividend-announced-by-
   massmutual

Company	2019 Dividends	2020 Dividends	2021 Dividends	2022 Dividends	2023 Dividends	2024 Est. Dividends
New York Life[15]	$1.8 billion	$1.9 billion	$1.8 billion	$1.9 billion	$2 billion	$2.2 billion
Northwestern Mutual[16]	$5.6 billion	$6 billion	$6.2 billion	$6.5 billion	$6.8 billion	$7.3 billion

These are great numbers and are the kind of numbers you want to see in an insurance company. This is great for both Checkers and Chess players. Checkers players, however, tend to stop there. Chess players, on the other hand, are busy looking under the hood and seeing how the insurance companies grew so fast and so well. Chess players will not only purchase the policies, but also use similar strategies to build their own wealth, albeit likely not on the same scale.

I emailed a leader at MassMutual, John Vaccaro, and I asked him, "How does a life insurance company like MassMutual have some of its best years during, and soon after, a global, life-threatening pandemic?"

He responded with, "I wish I could answer that in one sentence." He then sent me over to some marketing department who gave me a non-answer and wouldn't give me a direct explanation for this book.

---

15 https://www.newyorklife.com/newsroom/

16 https://news.northwesternmutual.com/

Doing a little research will give anyone the answer—MassMutual is diversifying its revenue across multiple different asset classes, which helps them ride out (and often succeed) in virtually any economic situation. It's not just them making those moves with their revenue, it's something that many great companies do.

DO WHAT YOU DO BEST

The whole point of this book is to show you that there is no one right answer, and you don't have to be pigeonholed into the same choices everyone around you is making. I know what it's like to be a Checkers player. I played that game when I was working as a police officer, investing a little of each check into my 457 plan (similar to a 401k plan), and that was pretty much the extent of my investment strategy.

But once I met wealthy people and learned they were playing Chess, I knew I wanted to play Chess. When my wife and I started shifting our game, we had a small amount of decent assets. Not a ton of free money to play with, but enough to get us started. If that's you, consider these things:

1. **Educate yourself on your options**. Real estate is one of the first strategies people should consider. You don't need an advanced degree to be a landlord. The average person can handle some rental properties. Real estate can create great, passive income. Start out with one property and gradually move to two or more.

2. **Know your leverage comfort level**. Once you know how much leverage you have (something we talk about in Chapter Six), look at your comfort level with using that leverage. Are you a big risk taker or someone who wants to play it safer?

3. **Build a team**. You need to have a good fiduciary financial advisor, tax professional, lender, etc. in your corner. They're the experts who are there to guide you. If you try to do this all on your own, you probably won't be successful. The experts are there to help you see any roadblocks that could potentially knock you off course.

4. **Master Checkers first**. Before you can jump right into playing Chess, you should become really great at Checkers because you can't buy a property or a business with charm. If you need a $100,000 down payment for a $500,000 property, you need to know where that $100,000 is coming from. As you shift from one game to the other, your attitude toward income-producing debt and taxes will undoubtedly change.

5. **Look to the future**. Don't buy into the whole "work like a dog making other people wealthy, giving you very little, and then retire and die hoping you don't run out of money" mantra. It is possible to build your income and assets so you can enjoy your life now as well as in the future. You should have a plan that not only allows you to retire and live comfortably, but to also leave a legacy of wealth for your heirs. Especially

if leaving a legacy for your family is important to you. No matter what, having a good team is essential.

Scale your game as you grow more comfortable with leverage. You don't have to own a hundred-unit apartment building or a hotel right off the bat (or ever). You don't have to own a hundred single family properties, either. You should have strategies to create passive or recurring income for you, whether that's from five properties or five hundred. That's what builds your Chess game and gets you closer to the level of wealth you want.

It's okay if you have a conservative financial personality and want to play Checkers. Like I've said before, it's a good game and can give you a decent retirement. There is no right or wrong financial personality. A more aggressive investor like me is going to pursue those opportunities that are helping the big dogs get bigger.

> ## The one thing you should not do is nothing. Doing nothing gets you nowhere.

If you have a financially conservative personality and just want to play Checkers, then fully fund those retirement plans and hope the market plays along with you, especially when you are getting closer to, and during, your retirement.

Conservative investors can also still play a good Chess game. In fact, sometimes the conservative investor (as far as their market-based assets go) will own residential real estate, multi-family real estate, and/or businesses. It's all about "owning doors," as it's called in the industry, as long as you are willing to use those market-based assets to create leverage for owning more.

A side note: There is a difference between multi-family properties that are considered commercial and ones that are considered residential properties. A multi-family commercial property has five or more units. Less than five, and it's a residential multi-family property.

There are also smart financial reasons for owning multi-family properties. If you own single family residences, the value of the residences you own is based on the other houses in that neighborhood. If you own a multi-family property, the value is based on the income derived from that property. That's why sometimes the multi-family property might work out better financially than buying a dozen single family properties.

Also think about the impact of economic fluctuations on single family homes verses multi-family properties. If you own individual properties and everything's value goes down at the same time (like in 2008) and you are overleveraged, you will likely be in trouble. However, during a crash like that, an apartment building may have been a better, safer investment because the value of the property is based on its income potential, not the apartment complex next to it.

Plus, when people rent when they can't afford to buy because everyone needs to live somewhere. In a neighborhood, your house is impacted by the value of the neighbor's houses, and if their houses go down in value so too does the amount you can sell your house for, which affects your profits. That's the difference in valuation for commercial real estate, which can sometimes be more dependable.

Systematic risk (meaning the whole darn market is going down) puts you on the edge of losing everything if the ship begins to sink. Diversification into different investments (especially income-producing assets) is the key to not losing your shirt when your, and everyone else's, market-based portfolios are going down.

It's important to do your research. Dig into the websites of these big companies and look at where they invest their profits. Start thinking like they do, and you will make money the way they do. Preferably all of the above.

Like I said earlier, you can also learn how to play a great Chess game by paying attention to the actions of the people who are where you want to be. A lot of people are still putting all their eggs in the stock market basket. If you're doing that, understand your why and how it will affect your wealth building. This book is designed, as I said, to be an overview of Chess and Checkers; we get into much deeper discussions about these strategies with the clients who work with our firm.

Whether you're investing in real estate, businesses, market-based assets, or other alternative investments, do what they do: keep moving forward and taking the risks you are comfortable with.

Because the only way to get to where you want to go from where you are today is to take that first step forward.

"What I admired most about [Bobby Fischer] was his ability to make what was in fact so difficult look easy to us. I try to emulate him."

— Magnus Carlsen

CHAPTER SIX

THERE'S LEVERAGE IN YOUR ANNUITIES

Before we start talking about how you can use your annuities to play a better Chess game, we first need to define what we mean by annuities in this context. That word can mean different things. One typical meaning that comes to mind for annuities are the financial products usually associated with insurance companies.

But for the purposes of this book, when we use the word "annuities," I am talking about income streams that are expected at the beginning or at the end of a time period (like rent to a landlord.) This is an "annuity due." Typically, these kinds of annuities put money in your pocket every month and don't have the same risks you might find in the stock market. They are also generally associated with cash-flowing assets.

Annuities due are basically an income stream you can pretty reliably count on receiving every single month. There are lots of variations—like licensing rights or royalties from something like this book—but the majority come from steady earning vehicles, like real estate and businesses. Like rent to a landlord, your mortgage payment is an annuity due to the bank.

Besides not having to physically trade hours for dollars like you would at a job in order to earn them, why would you want these types of annuities? They provide something possibly just as valuable than income:

Leverage.

Leverage is your ability to borrow money. In essence, leverage allows individuals or businesses to control a larger asset base or investment than they could otherwise afford. The more things you own, the more collateral you have to borrow money and buy investments that will generate income to repay the loans.

You aren't technically repaying the loan out of your pocket because the income generated from the asset you bought is what repays the loan. Municipalities use this type of borrowing in the form of revenue bonds, such as the ones they put out for building a toll road (something we discussed in Chapter Three). They issue the bonds, borrow the money, build the road, and then use the money from the tolls to repay the bonds, plus the interest. Hospitals can also be funded in this way.

When you have the ability to borrow, you are in a position of power and can make many more, and sometimes bigger, financial moves. Most of us have already used the leverage our job income gives us to get a mortgage. Without that leverage, how long would it have taken you to save the money and buy the home outright with cash? Would you have *ever* been able to do that? By having leverage, either from your assets or the income from your employment, the bank was willing to give you the mortgage to buy the house.

When you have leverage, you have breathing room if you need to take on a loan or some kind of financing. When you have leverage, your risks are mitigated, and you are operating from a place of greater financial security.

Leverage, however, only works for you when you're not afraid to use it. But when you do, you're now playing Chess, not Checkers.

THE DANGER OF A SCARCITY MINDSET

When it comes to money, however, people are unfortunately often operating in a scarcity mindset instead of an abundance mindset. Which mindset you choose can make a *big* difference in your results.

A scarcity mindset is when someone thinks there's not enough for everyone. There's only so much pie out there, and you better get a slice right now or you will miss out on pie forever, or worse, believe they can't even get a sliver for themselves. An abundance mindset, on the other hand, believes there is pie everywhere, available for everyone, and you can have as many slices as you want. Especially if you are willing to do the things necessary to get that slice.

A scarcity mindset can cause you to panic, to get in over your head, and end up in a dangerous financial position. People with a scarcity mindset are typically buying properties and counting solely on their day job income to pay off the loan. There are multiple problems in doing that. One, you only receive so much income from your job. Two, if you lose your job, the bank is holding the house as collateral on the loan. If you stop making the payments, the bank will likely take the house back. You can easily get in serious financial trouble that way.

People who operate in that manner are rolling the dice every single day on their boss not firing them. They also might think cutting out things will drastically improve their situation. Here's the truth: avoiding Starbucks a few times a week is not likely to change your financial position. You're just going to change your cinnamon latte intake.

However, if you are receiving income from more than one source and lose one, you still have the other sources to pay back the loan. That allows you to work from a more abundant mindset because you are not dependent solely on one avenue. You are, as I said earlier, diversified in income.

I've met many people who want to move to that next level of financial growth, but their scarcity mindset tells them they can't afford it, they shouldn't take risks, and that it's too scary to do something like that. They also can be influenced by well-meaning loved ones who unwittingly reinforce that scarcity mindset. I get it; it's tough to ignore advice from people who love you, but that's sometimes what you have to do. Spouses, parents, family members, and close friends think they are helping you by sending up caution flags like these: "Don't take that risk. What if it doesn't work out? What if you lose everything?" It's not that they don't want you to have nice things or to grow your wealth. Their fears of loss bleed over into their heartfelt advice, which can affect your decision making.

It *is* scary to make big financial purchases. If it wasn't, everyone would do it. In my opinion, though, the best way to create generational wealth is to take some of those risks—but to do so from a strategic and confident position instead of with a scarcity mindset.

No scenario is perfect, and there will always be hiccups along the way, but if you create an income stream that doesn't require you to manage it day to day, then you open doors to even bigger possibilities.

I'm not talking about the annuity payments you receive from insurance products. In that case, you're making a bet that you're going to live an extremely long life, while the financial institution is using long-standing statistics that say you're going to die at a certain age. The way you win that bet is to outlive the initial payment from the annuity by living to a biblical age.

So, how do you escape that place of scarcity and trade it for a place that typically offers more security? Or even better, start to create that abundance mindset in yourself? The answer is pretty simple: Purchase assets that produce regular income streams, like preschools.

THE ACCIDENTAL PRESCHOOL INVESTOR

Last year, my wife and I were looking for a business to invest in as part of our Chess strategy to produce an additional annuity due (income stream). Over the years, this approach has allowed us to purchase multiple properties and start businesses, building regular income and generational wealth. We looked into this investment for multiple reasons: we wanted something that could be passed on to our children or sold by our children after we were gone, and we wanted to expand beyond rental properties and into small businesses.

We started looking at different franchises, weighing the pros and cons of each. Our criteria were that the business had to produce good income and provide value to the community.

In the beginning of that process, I called someone I knew who owned a preschool and asked him if he knew of any franchise brokers who could help me with my search. He told me that he didn't know much about franchise brokers; he only knew the world of preschools.

At the time, we didn't even think of preschools as an option. They weren't even on our radar. A couple of months later, however, we wound up purchasing a preschool from a person who headhunts franchises. We got involved in that industry because they are an "evergreen" business that can make a fabulous kind of annuity/income stream and deliver value by providing education to children.

We didn't know much about preschools but, after researching the market, we realized that schools are a business that yield positive gains with confidence. There's always a need in the market for quality preschools, and parents are unlikely to stop spending on their children's education when the economy takes a dive. They'll cut the maid or the lawn service before they cut out education. That, to us, is a business that makes sense.

So, we bought a preschool from a franchisor and added it to the things that bring our family regularly recurring revenue. For the most part, the preschool will be hands-off, because we are hiring the right people to run the day-to-day operation and allow us to deal with the business side.

These are called semi-absentee businesses. There are fully-absentee businesses out there (like vending machines), but no business, in my opinion, is ever 100% absentee. You need to do your homework, study the numbers, and hire the right people to run the operation.

The business you buy needs to create positive cashflow, so it's crucial to hire people who know what they're doing and whom you can trust. I believe it's also important to pay your employees as much as you can, not just the market rate. The market rate allows businesses, especially corporations, to take a lot of value away from their people by paying very little and, also, charging very little. Yes, it's important that the business makes a substantial amount of money so you can purchase additional businesses that create more jobs that pay well, but it's also important to take care of good employees.

It's the same with rental properties. In my opinion, none of those are 100% hands-off, either because things break or tenants move out, which means you either have to fix it yourself or find someone who can. I think your goal should be to build a team of property managers and repair people who can keep things running smoothly, minimizing your hands-on time.

THEN WHAT?

Each of these income streams is designed to do one thing—help you play a bigger and better Chess game. Growing your income and wealth to a level that allows you to not only take care of your family, but also your children's families, and so on. That kind of financial freedom is often found in passive income streams derived from rental properties or recurring income streams such as businesses and other investments.

I understand that it's a pretty scary leap to make, especially if you've been playing Checkers all your life—even if you've been playing a pretty aggressive game. There is no perfect scenario for when and how to take that first leap, but there are ways to make your decision more successful, like by thinking of your moves as connecting boards in a bridge.

In pretty much every scenario of river-crossing, it's smarter to build a bridge, rather than just jumping off the cliff and hope you have enough strength to get you to the other side. It's the same with financial moves. Build a bridge a little at a time instead of just diving off the cliff. Nobody wants to miscalculate and take a thirty-story tumble. There may be times when your bridge is as rickety as the one in *Indiana Jones* but, once you start building it, your bridge will strengthen with each and every income stream you add.

Then you are approaching these situations from a position of power and an abundance mindset instead of a scarcity mindset. You aren't solely trying to make it on your paycheck nor are you terrified of losing your job. You have that bridge beneath you for support if something falls apart or doesn't come through. That bridge, no matter how narrow, makes it a lot easier for you to take the next step toward playing a bigger and better Chess game.

> The first rental property or small business you own might not deliver much cash flow. You might think it's not even worth it. Try to look at the big picture—that each of those properties and businesses bring you one step closer to where you want to be.

That first property or business can be like a faucet that starts dripping a few drops an hour. It can take a while to fill your cup with water, but the more it drips, the more water you have, and the trickle becomes a tiny pour. Before you know it, it feels like there's an endless amount of water coming out of the faucet. In your abundance mindset, you know you'll never be thirsty again—if you do it right.

You probably don't want to go overboard and buy ten rental properties or a dozen businesses at once because it may be too difficult to manage and overwhelm you. Also, you are more likely to make mistakes that can cost you "tuition," in the form of financial losses. If you're like me, you want to pay the lowest amount of tuition possible. Making a small mistake on a smaller investment is a lot easier to swallow than making that same mistake on a large investment because that error will cost you a lot more money. As you learn and grow, take the next step and add the next section to your bridge when you feel confident and have the income stream to support it.

You don't have to buy one or the other, or even both. Buy what you feel comfortable with, but buy *something*. Imagine this strategy like playing Monopoly®. You get your $1500 in startup capital, then go around the board without buying *any* property. Maybe you're hoping to save up for a prime property like Boardwalk or Park Place. In the meantime, your competitors are actively acquiring properties, including the "less-desirable" ones like Mediterranean and Baltic—and making money every time you pay them rent, which slowly depletes the cash you have on hand to create your property monopoly. If you pay enough rent, you can't afford to buy any properties at all. You're not very likely to win the game if you do that.

Whether it's real estate, businesses, or market-based investments, the concept is the same: seize opportunities when they arise. Saving up for a potentially better opportunity in the future might be a risky endeavor, akin to hoping for the perfect property in Monopoly. In the dynamic landscape of investments, acting on the opportunities presented may often be the wiser choice, ensuring you're actively participating and building your portfolio rather than waiting for some perfect moment that may never come.

When you're looking for a business to buy, keep in mind that it doesn't have to be something hot and trendy. Most of those plain, old, "boring" businesses, like preschools and laundromats, can be great investments because they tend to be recession-proof. Look at the risks and rewards of the business you are buying to be sure that it is most likely to make money no matter what happens to the economy.

While businesses are great cash flow generators, your long-term plan should involve real estate. Companies come and go, technology changes things, and industries wax and wane, but real estate is something that will always be in demand. The population is only increasing (according to Worldometer, about twice as many people are being born each day, compared to how many are dying[17]) and that means there will always be a need for housing.

Because there is one simple fact that will always be true: People *really* don't like to be cold at night.

CHANGING THE MINDSET

I went to St. Anthony's High School, one of the best schools in New York, but I always felt like the goal of high school was to get into a good college. That was my job in high school, and once I got into a good college (which ended up being Belmont Abbey College), my job was to get a really good job

---

17 https://www.worldometers.info/#google_vignette

with great benefits. Nowhere was it prominent in the guidance office that these other options existed with recurring income or entrepreneurship.

My childhood mindset wasn't on playing Chess. No one even talked to me about that. My whole goal was to go from one traditional choice to another, and it would have been very easy to stay stuck in that mindset and constantly worry about getting a paycheck. I've met literally thousands of people who are caught in that same thought pattern. Changing people's mindsets is the whole reason why I wrote this book. That starts when our kids are young.

In our house, we don't even use the word *job* now. I ask my kids: *What kind of business do you want to own? What kind of real estate would you like to own?* When she was four years old, my daughter told me she wanted to own a car dealership. That wasn't something we influenced, but rather a goal she came up with on her own. She was also clear that she didn't want to work there every day, but instead own it and hire the right people. Because we had taught her the pie is limitless, even in preschool, she was working with an abundance mindset.

My son wants to take over my wealth advisory practice after, of course, he's done playing in the Major Leagues. He also has that "pie-is-available-for-all" mindset. To learn more, he recently took a business class in middle school. He was initially excited about it, but the class turned out to be more about learning Microsoft Word, Excel, and other software programs used in the workforce. In my opinion, these aren't necessarily the elements you need to run a good business. Those skills are the kind of thing business owners hire other people for. The class didn't go over balance sheets, profit and loss statements, capital injections, or any of the business class pillars. But that's okay. He's only in middle school. He has plenty of time to learn about those things, and to build an abundance mindset.

I was once a hardcore Checkers player, working my butt off and putting in tons of overtime at the police department. I was trading hours for dollars at the cost of relationships and, basically, any kind of life.

Then I started meeting people who weren't working forty hours a week, plus overtime, like I was and yet they were doing really well financially. They said things like, "There are legal ways to not pay a lot in taxes." That intrigued me. I wanted to know the how and what of their strategies—so I could do the same.

That was when I began understanding how active income works and how passive income could really change my future.

KNOW THE DIFFERENCE

Most of us just think about "income" in general. We don't even pause to think about different types or how we could be earning income in different ways, some of which don't require hours of backbreaking work.

ACTIVE INCOME:

What It Is: This is the money you earn by actively working, like your paycheck from your job. Example: If you work at a company and get paid $50,000 a year, that is your active income.

PASSIVE INCOME:

What It Is: This is money you earn without actively working (not "materially participating"), like from limited partnerships in businesses or rental properties. Example: If you own a rental property and receive $1,000 a month from rent, that's passive income. You make money without having to trade hours of your life for dollars.

PORTFOLIO INCOME:

What It Is: This is money you make from your investments, like stocks or bonds. It's a bit like the profit you get when you sell something you invested in. This is commonly referred to as a capital gain. Example: If you bought stocks for $1,000 and later sold them for $1,500, the $500 you made is a capital gain.

TAX IMPLICATIONS FOR EACH

Taxes are an inevitable part of life, which is why it's so important to understand them and where they will cost you the most. The more you know, the more you can, essentially, save on paying Uncle Sam.

> *Active Income:* The money you get from working is usually taxed at the progressive, regular rates, and your employer takes some of those taxes out of your paychecks.

> *Passive Income:* Money you make from things like rental properties or certain investments might have different tax rules. Depending on the type of income you receive, you might pay taxes on it differently (if it's offset by an asset loss) and, in some cases, not at all.

> *Portfolio Income:* The money you make from selling investments may have special tax rates. For instance, if you held onto your stocks for a long time before selling, you may pay lower taxes than if you held onto it for a short time. "Long time" is usually defined as a year and a day.

In everyday terms, passive income is like the golden ticket for income from a tax perspective. In addition, if you hit a rough patch and lose money one year, you might be able to use those losses to lower taxes on future wins. Remember, the government *wants* you to invest.

The best part? Passive income often means less work compared to a regular job. It's like having your money work for you while you enjoy more free time, which sounds like a great deal all the way around. I can take my son to a baseball game and earn money at the same time. However, the tax implications can get tricky, so having a chat with the tax expert on your team is a smart move to ensure you're making the most of your income.

When I decided to do what the wealthy people I met were doing, I started learning everything I could because I wanted a lifestyle where I didn't have to worry about losing my job (and then losing my house). As a police officer, I had a pretty guaranteed job, but I knew I would eventually retire from that career and wanted something that would give me steady returns on my investment and be less risky than just blindly picking stocks. I wanted financial security and dependability, which is achievable with a diversification of the assets you buy.

I went back to what I love to do—talk finance and baseball. I wasn't going to be involved in the Major Leagues anytime soon (or ever), but I could talk to people about financial options, learn as much as I could, and then apply that information to my own life. I knew the more I changed my income streams from active to passive, the lower my tax burden would be because of all the things we talked about in Chapter Three.

I'm not just giving you information—I am actively doing the things I talk about in this book. I started out taking calculated strategies that were low-risk/low-reward options. Building my bridge, one plank at a time. As those began to earn, I invested money into things that were slightly riskier, and so on and so forth. I gradually moved from playing Checkers to playing Chess until I put those Checkers pieces away forever.

One day, I received a really cool compliment from someone I knew growing up. I was sitting down with her and her husband for dinner. We started chatting about money and she said, "I want to listen to you because I know you, I know where you're from, I know what you had, and somehow you were the one to get out of the matrix. What I want to know now is how you did it." She was super-smart in school, very likely went to a good college, worked a job like most of us, but was now ready to learn how to play Chess.

You can do that, too. It all starts with your mindset and the belief that you have what it takes to build a stronger, better bridge that will carry you to the other side.

"It doesn't matter how strong a player you are, if you fail to register some development in the opening, then you are asking for trouble."

— John Emms

CHAPTER SEVEN

COVERING YOUR LIABILITIES WITH YOUR ASSETS

Remember your first car? I mean the first one you bought with your own money, the first one you "owned" (of course the bank probably had a lien on it). I bought my first car when I was twenty-one, a Nissan Sentra, with an interest rate of 12% because I had no credit history. I didn't have bad credit; I had *no* credit, so I ended up with a high-interest loan.

At the time, I was lucky to have a job that allowed me to pay off the car early, but most people are not that lucky. A lot of us who go through the car-buying process when we're not making a whole lot of money or aren't a strong credit candidate (like I was at that time) end up paying a lot of money in interest for the car itself. In this scenario, the bank obviously earns money from your monthly car payment in the form of interest. But what if it could work out the other way around?

This car scenario is something pretty much everyone is familiar with, but we're going to use it to illustrate the concept of covering your liabilities with your assets. If you can understand and master doing that on a small scale, with a car, then you can easily scale those principles to assets with far more value. We're starting with something simple, a process most people have gone through, and showing you how to use that same concept to buy a yacht, take lavish vacations, buy a second home, jewelry…you get the point. These things are not necessarily going to give you income, but they are things that you enjoy or consider a necessity, like a vehicle.

KNOW YOUR CAR PURCHASING MENTALITY

People generally buy cars in one of two ways: they finance or lease it. If you finance a car, you're paying interest on a vehicle that is depreciating (but not the good kind of depreciation) from the minute you drive it off the lot. At the end of the loan period, the car is worth a whole lot less than when you bought it, and all the money you paid in interest is gone. If you're leasing a car, you're making all those payments and at the end of the lease period, you own…nothing.

Neither of these are a good way to help you build wealth, but you *can* use your car purchase mindset to get you closer to building your wealth. The thing to understand about a car loan is who wins in that equation—the bank. Because of the interest, they know you will pay them a set interest amount for the number of years of the loan. That's a win for the bank, but not necessarily for you. So, what do you do if you know you're going to need another car soon? There are some financial pundits who say save up some cash while driving a clunker. Save the money in a good interest-bearing or brokerage account, and then pay cash for the car. I think this can work out well for pretty much anyone playing Checkers. If you are saving the car "payment" you would have made (had you bought a car) every month in a brokerage account, you're gaining interest on the money you would have been paying to the bank. Once you have enough money saved to buy the car outright, purchase it. But—and this is key for continuing that forward momentum—keep making those same "payments" back to your brokerage account and keep earning interest on that money while you are driving your new car. Rinse and repeat several years later.

When you continue to make the car "payments" to yourself into a brokerage account, you are the beneficiary of the interest the account is bearing because it stays with you instead of going to the bank. In my opinion, this is infinitely better than just financing a car. Again, this is a great Checkers move, if that's the game you're playing. If you want to play Chess, however, you need to make some different moves.

WHAT CHESS PLAYERS DO TO BUY A CAR

The Chess move would be to drive that clunker even longer while you are saving those "payments." When you have enough money to buy a car, you don't buy a car yet.

Wait, what? Yes, exactly that. You don't buy a car *yet*.

You buy an *asset* that will generate cash flow for you—maybe a rental property. When you buy that property and start collecting rent, it delivers money to you, which is a definite win for your game. You want to create enough of a cash flow to pay the mortgage and pay your monthly car payment for the car you don't have—yet.

Let me give you an example. Don't focus on the numbers, just the concepts. I know different real estate markets and interest rates affect everything I'm about to say. The numbers below are purely for easy math purposes.

For instance, let's say you save $800 a month until you have $40,000, and use that $40,000 to purchase a $200,000 rental property (which could be in another state, far away). Your mortgage payment is $1500, but you are collecting $2300 a month in rent. Further, let's subtract $200 a month for taxes and insurance on the property, which gives you a "car payment" of $600 a month.

Now you can go get a car loan. I know, that's the opposite of what I just said, but this situation is not the same as the good

Checkers play. Now you have an asset that is producing cash flow—enough to pay back the bank every month.

The $2300 in rent covers the mortgage and your car payment, which means you don't have to come up with the interest or principal for the car loan out of your own pocket. The bank still gets its money, but you have a rental property paying all those bills for you. Essentially, you are paying the bank with someone else's money.

> ## Now we're playing Chess, folks!

Your liability (the car) is covered by the asset (rental property). At the end of five years (the term of a typical car loan), you still have all your money in the equity of the home (during reasonable economic times) and a car that's paid off. If this works out perfectly—and remember, there are probably going to be bumps in the road—all your money is still with you and the property you purchased probably appreciated in value.

> ## Your balance sheet is going up and you're building wealth.

Ideally, the rental payments are more than the combined total of the mortgage and car payment. Then you're making money while owning those two assets, a Chess move that has great potential payoffs for you.

I've explained this strategy to auto salespeople in the past and it shocked some of them because it's not what they normally hear from a customer. A couple of years ago, my truck was having a lot of costly issues. We loved our 2002 Yukon XL and even named it Gus. When the kids were small, we took it everywhere—from Texas to Florida to Maine—because it could carry a lot of stuff. It even had a tape deck with an adapter that could plug into the phone's audio output (back when phones had those) and a CD player.

We loved every minute of the 200,000 miles we put on Gus— until so many things went wrong and he had to go. RIP Gus.

So, I went to a dealership to buy a new, not nearly as cool or rugged, SUV. The salesman noticed I was constantly on my phone. I didn't want to be rude by being on the phone while he was speaking, so I told him, "I'm listening to you, I'm just trying to communicate with one of my realtors in Jacksonville, Florida while we do this deal."

"Are you buying a house and moving?" he asked.

"No," I said, "I'm buying a house because I don't want to pay for this car loan with my own money. I'll pay you back with the rent from the house I'm purchasing right now." That day in the dealership, I worked out a deal to buy a small rental property at the same time I was buying a new SUV. That rental property covered my car payment and gave me a little extra cash every month. Which is great, I must say.

THINK MUCH BIGGER

If you're playing Chess, you want to take that same strategy and use it on a bigger scale. Meaning, don't just buy liabilities (like cars and boats) that depreciate right away; instead, buy more assets that can continue to increase your cash flow, *then* purchase the liability. A little rental property can cover your Chevy Traverse, a large hotel can cover your $20 million yacht. It's all the same concept.

If you are covering the cost of those liabilities with your assets, and the money to pay those loans is coming from another asset source, it doesn't feel like you're paying anything at all. That's a *really* nice feeling.

I know it can be tough because we're so used to having everything we want and having it right now (probably along with some bone-crushing debt). Just think long-term and big-picture. Drive that one car until you can save a boatload of money, make that monthly payment to yourself the whole time, and have the guts to buy the asset first instead of buying the car.

It can be scary if this is your first time doing this. There are a lot of unknowns and what-ifs. But here's the truth—your chances of building generational wealth are very, very slim if you play Checkers. Chess is the game that gets you there if that's what you want.

What if the renters default? No question, this happens from time to time. The key is to have enough cash reserves to handle those types of risks. Don't use your last dollar to buy an asset and pray nothing happens. Use that savings but set aside enough in reserve to cover the unforeseeable expenses, like a new roof or three months of no rent. Leave those reserves in your brokerage account (so they keep earning interest) and save them for any emergencies.

> ## It's about having the money but not using the money.

DON'T DO THIS BROKE

Every time there's another real estate boom, thousands of people try to get in on the action by purchasing real estate or get into some weird real estate-oriented scheme (which is probably even worse).

The problem? They don't have any money. There are plenty of videos on YouTube about how to buy real estate with no money down, but this is the kind of risky move that can get you into big trouble. Without reserves (or equity in the property), you have zero options if something goes wrong.

That's not to say you need to be a multi-millionaire to buy property. Far from it. One of my jobs as a wealth advisor is to help my clients look very, very good on paper to a lender but still make sure they are in a strong financial position to handle things that could go wrong. Because that's where the rubber meets the road in Chess—using the lender's money to purchase the assets but always having the ability to pay the lender back if you need to.

This "game" —saving your money, taking out loans, purchasing the asset, receiving income from that asset, putting some of that income back into the savings pot, and putting some into your pocket to enjoy your life (all while continuing to grow this strategy)—is the best way, in my opinion, to achieve the kind of wealth that is going to change your financial trajectory.

When you use these leveraging strategies, you no longer look at the bank as evil; they are a *partner* in your deals. Your business partner, in a way. Yes, they receive the interest on the mortgage or business loans, but you benefit from the rent income you deposit into your bank account. Some of that money goes to the principle and some to the bank as interest. In the end, you are the one who benefits from the capital appreciation when property values rise.

Tax-wise, it's even better: You get 100% of the appreciation of the home's value *and* 100% of the depreciation allowed for that home come tax time. Again, that's because the government wants to encourage people to invest in real estate. When you sell that property and buy another one that is the same value or higher, you're also deferring capital gains taxes, which is another win for you. If you never sell and let the property keep appreciating, it becomes a win for your descendants.

Look at what the mutual fund companies (investment companies) are investing in and where they are putting your money. There's a reason the largest buildings in any major metropolitan city are usually banks, whether that be commercial or investment banks. The banks are investing the money you invested in them into real estate and different businesses and assets, so that the bank can reap the benefits of those investments.

Why more people aren't mimicking the successful Chess moves major corporations make is an enigma to me. Most people continue to live paycheck to paycheck and don't even have an emergency fund. The only way to get from there to here is by changing your mindset.

Start by learning to play Checkers really, really well:

- Definitely have an emergency fund.
- Get the life insurance and other insurances you need.
- Invest in a brokerage account and retirement accounts.
- Have a college savings plan.
- Save before you buy; and when you buy, buy strategically.

Then, when you realize you want to make better financial moves, you can start by unlearning a lot of what you have already learned (yes, that's another Yoda reference). Look at each move, like the car example I talked about, as a bridge to move from playing Checkers to Chess. Simply paying cash for the car is a far better financial move than just getting a car loan; but using that savings to purchase an asset that pays for itself, and the car becomes a *wealth-building financial move.*

One move at a time gets you to a totally different position on the board and gives you the kind of financial freedom you've been dreaming about for years.

"Once there is the slightest suggestion of combinational possibilities on the board, look for unusual moves. Apart from making your play creative and interesting, it will help you get better results."

—Alexander Kotov

CHAPTER EIGHT

WEALTH IS NOT A PRODUCT ON THE SHELF

The moment that changed everything for me, especially the way I look at business value, happened on a double-decker tour bus in Miami and had to do with some palm trees. It was 2012, and my wife and I had left the cold winter in Virginia to vacation in Miami (I believe it was also our first vacation without the kids).

As our luck would have it, it was also cold in Florida, not Florida-cold (which is like 70 degrees), but Virginia-cold, which meant we didn't want to go to the beach because it would be even colder there with the wind coming in off the Atlantic. I didn't know it ever got that cold in Miami!

Instead, we decided to spend the afternoon on a tour bus that would take us around Star Island, a man-made island in Biscayne Bay that is full of wealthy residents. We were, by far, the youngest people on that bus by about three decades.

We were sitting on the top level of this double-decker bus, driving past all the mansions where wealthy people lived. "That's Will Smith's house there," the tour guide said. "Elizabeth Taylor has a house over there. And there's Shaquille O'Neal's home." Everyone oohed and aahed and snapped pictures of the celebrity life.

Then we drove by a sprawling mansion that literally stretched the entire length of the back side of the island. "Whose house is *THAT*?" someone asked.

"If I said his name," the tour guide said with a twinkle in her eye, "you probably wouldn't know who he is. But I'll give you a clue. If you look at the palm trees surrounding his house, you'll see that they are the tallest and the stiffest on the island."

She paused a beat. Waited for us to make the connection.

Then she said, "That's the house of Philip Frost. He's the guy who invented Viagra."

The whole bus broke out in giggles like you'd hear in a schoolyard because the tree reference was a pretty good joke. Then, a man, who was probably in his late sixties, stood up in the back of the bus and shouted extremely loudly, "He deserves every inch of that house!" People laughed and applauded and cheered for Philip Frost.

As I looked on, I realized the people on this bus, people who were nowhere near as wealthy as Philip Frost, were totally okay with Mr. Frost being a wealthy man with a huge house because he brought value to their lives, particularly the guy in the back of the bus.

> When people feel like you're making money off their suffering, they're resentful of your wealth. When you deliver value to their lives, they're usually genuinely happy for you.

It's a lot like when you do things that make the government happy (which we talked about in Chapter Three) and are rewarded with tax incentives. A big developer who builds much-needed affordable housing or who builds a preschool in an area that doesn't have one provides value to the area. People want to see someone like that succeed because their own lives are being enriched by what the wealthy person is doing. Amazon, for instance, is a massive conglomerate that makes Jeff Bezos incredibly rich, but few people begrudge Bezos that financial reward because he has made their lives easier by delivering almost whatever they need in a day or two.

That's the key to creating long-lasting wealth: bringing value to the people around you. It's not about being Scrooge McDuck and swimming in gold coins. It's about enhancing the well-being of your life and the lives of others.

Speaking of Scrooge McDuck, he does a pretty good job of explaining wealth-building to Huey, Dewey, and Louie in the cartoon from the 1960s. Look it up on YouTube.

KNOW WHAT WEALTH MEANS TO YOU

The word wealth— an old English word—is derived from the word "weal" which meant "well-being" or "welfare." Back then, people used it as an adjective to describe someone who possessed those qualities. To our ancestors, wealth wasn't about the money—it was about life satisfaction.

To me, wealth is an accumulation of valuable things (like property) that can be used to increase your ability to borrow, something which ultimately has the best value because it gives you choices, freedom, and opportunities to further increase your wealth. It gives you peace of mind because you no longer live paycheck to paycheck. It gives you a legacy to leave your kids. It gives you the resources to go after your dreams.

The big Chess players use those accumulated things (properties, stocks, businesses) as leverage to get loans to buy more valuable things, whether that is art or apartments. That accumulated wealth gives the bank confidence in your repayment abilities, which then gives the bank the confidence to invest in other areas.

Richard Branson, in his book, *Screw It, Let's Do It,* tells a story about the time he got really well dressed and showed up at the bank. The banker immediately realized that Branson was in financial trouble because he wasn't wearing his usual shorts and sandals. The bank still loaned the money to Branson because he had been able to deliver and perform on his previous loans, and the bank was willing to continue to bet on his ability to do that again.

You don't have to be Stephen King to be a successful author, and you don't have to be Richard Branson to be a successful investor. You can play Chess on a much smaller scale and make life a little better for your kids than you had it when you were growing up. Each subsequent generation can improve the life of the ones to follow.

The fact that my parents played a really great game of Checkers with their money allowed me to have more financial freedom with my choices because I won't have to clean up any of their money messes. There is no towering debt left for me to pay off or an upside-down mortgage. They invested well enough to fund their retirement, which gives me the ability to go after my own goals.

I didn't grow up with a silver spoon—quite the opposite. I remember being a little kid and going to the Salvation Army to pick out clothes. I also remember eating the government cheese that came in the brown box in the early 80s (I still think that cheese makes *the best* grilled cheese sandwiches). My parents worked very hard, trading those hours for dollars, to take care of us, send me to a great high school, and build their retirement. They started with very little but kept improving our lives as the years went by.

Not everyone is going to start off in the same place, but that doesn't mean you can't improve where you are now and where your kids are as you go forward. I realize that many people do have to help their parents out financially. If that's the case, you can still play a great game of Checkers or Chess because you have many of the tools in your hands right now. The access to information has never been better than it is today; you can learn just about anything with an Internet connection and a cheap laptop or smartphone.

WHAT WILL MAKE YOU HAPPY?

While having money makes paying the bills a whole lot easier, it doesn't mean you'll be happy. Multiple studies have shown that people who make around $100,000 a year are pretty happy, overall.[18] Making more money didn't multiply their happiness.

Happiness is found in knowing where you want to be and reaching that level. If you are never quite happy, no matter how much money you have in the bank, or always thinking, "I'll be happy when I do this. No, when I do that," then happiness is going to elude you, probably forever.

If you are living the life you dreamed of when you were a kid and are able to spend your time doing things you enjoy,

---

18 https://www.cnbc.com/2023/03/28/how-your-salary-affects-happiness.html

then happiness should be the natural byproduct. If not, then maybe take another look at where you place your focus.

Some people suffer from lifestyle grief and are either always mourning the life they had or mourning the fact that they never had a particular life. That's not healthy. You end up constantly chasing your tail, spending more and more money, and thinking that will work—but it never really does.

That's why I encouraged you to imagine your ideal future in the beginning of the book. Once you reach that place, take a look around and gauge your happiness level. Hopefully, it's high.

That's not to say you have to be *satisfied*. Some people always want another challenge. They charge out of bed to take on a new adventure or to reach the next goal. Those people can be happy with their life but not be *satisfied* with what they are doing or happy with their progress. They might want to keep expanding, keep growing, or start moving into other areas, and that's totally fine.

My son has learned this lesson through practicing baseball and working to get better at the sport. I tell him that it's okay to be dissatisfied with where he is right now, but to always be happy with all of the improvements he's making and, most of all, with the game itself. The goal for me with these lessons is not to raise a Major League baseball player (although that would be totally awesome); my goal is to raise a successful and kind businessman. Baseball is just a tool for those lessons.

DO YOU WANT TO BE GOOD? OR GREAT?

Jim Collins, author of the book *Good to Great*, once said, "Good is the enemy of great." What he means is that when you settle for good enough, you stop striving to be great. It's completely okay to be satisfied with good—just know that means you are very unlikely to ever be great. Plenty of people have built wonderful lives by striving for good. There's absolutely nothing wrong with that.

Envy, however, will steal your joy faster than anything else. If you strive to be great, but are envious of others, it will only undermine your progress if you constantly envy the person with a nicer house or newer car. There will *always* be someone with nicer stuff.

When I started doing all this, I sat down and looked at what made me happy. Besides my family, talking finance and baseball make me ridiculously happy. I could do nothing else all day besides finance and baseball and family time and go through life very happy. I don't have to be the richest person in the world to have that happiness. But I definitely want to have enough money to build a life that allows me to focus on finance and baseball, and leave that same freedom to my kids.

That's really where you should start when you begin to think about what wealth looks like to you. Does your image of wealth include an Audi and a house in Monte Carlo? Does it include more time with your family and less time working?

Or does it include a comfortable life that makes you excited to jump out of bed every day?

That definition is important to know as you go on this journey and remember to hold onto that as you make decisions in the future. You can't just buy wealth on Amazon (yet) because it's not a product; and even if it were, the term means different things to different people. Being "wealthy" has a different look for you than it does for your neighbor or your cousin. If you talk to a hundred people, you'll get a hundred different answers on what amount of money classifies wealth to them.

We'd all love to be billionaires overnight, but the chances of that are 1 in 292 *million* if you are playing the Powerball. If you're playing Chess, the chances are rare as well, even for those who play Chess pretty well. In my opinion, Chess players can easily become multi-millionaires, but not necessarily billionaires.

That's because we all know no one goes out, buys a pair of running shoes, and immediately runs the Boston Marathon. They train, they build up their mileage, their strength, their mental endurance. They figure out what methods work for them and which ones don't. They make mistakes, they fall down—

And they get back up again and return to running.

Accept the fact that, at some point, you will probably lose money doing this, at least temporarily. No one likes losing money, not even billionaires. You need to know where your comfort level resides. If your livelihood isn't hanging in the balance of how well you play Chess (and it shouldn't be), then there should be an X number of dollars that you are willing to lose (and capable of losing). In finance, this is called your risk capacity.

Warren Buffet's number-one rule is, "Don't lose money." But if you asked him, I'm sure he'd be able to tell you about his strikeouts because *everyone* has them. The funny thing about successful people is that we can tell you more about our strikeouts than we can our hits.

This isn't the same as going to the casino and losing money at the roulette table. This is about things going wrong, whether that's due to an economic crash or a hurricane or something else.

If you aren't in a strong financial position when a loss happens, then you're just going to end up continually throwing Hail Mary passes down the field. Unless you have Gronk waiting on the other end to catch the ball, that kind of risky move could eventually wipe you out. Even Gronk couldn't make a crucial catch against the Giants in a championship game. That's why it's best to have a set amount in mind that you will be financially okay with losing, just in case.

You'd be mad for a few days at losing that money, but it wouldn't be the end of the world. Knowing that number will help you get comfortable with being uncomfortable.

> Taking risks can be scary.
> Making mistakes can be costly.
> But what is it costing you to
> do neither of those things?
> There's a risk in doing nothing, too.

I've met a lot of people who have made good money playing Chess, and nearly all of them have said, "I wish I started bigger from the jump."

My response is simple. "You didn't, and that is probably one of the reasons why you are extremely successful now. You didn't just swing for the fences the first time you had an at bat." By making calculated, strategic moves and adding risk as you are ready for it, you can be far more successful than just diving in head-first.

You're going to make mistakes; that's inevitable. Think of your mistakes like your tuition in college. The mistakes you make are going to teach you more than pretty much anything you can read or hear. They will teach you what works for you... and what doesn't. They will teach you how far you can leap... and how quickly you can get across the divide. Mistakes are great (as long as you don't keep making the same ones over and over). Basically, if you're not making mistakes, you're not doing enough or risking enough.

There are also a few questions you can ask yourself to help you decide how far you want to leap off the cliff when you start out playing Chess:

1. **How much risk tolerance do you have?** Are you retiring next year or in forty years? Do you have a panic attack at the thought of big purchases or are you okay with taking a few risks? Just because this person is doing A doesn't mean you have to do A, too. Sometimes you can play excellent Chess by choosing to make move B. Know your risk tolerance level and play accordingly.

2. **Is your financial advisor doing the same things?** As a wealth advisor, I don't want to be judged solely on rates of return. If I could just spin straw into gold, I'd do that all day, but I can't, so I play Chess instead. I want my clients to look at how their lifestyles have improved because they have worked with me and made the moves I advised. If your financial advisor has been with you for a long time but your lifestyle hasn't improved in all those years, it might be time to find another financial advisor. Do they take their own advice? Like I mentioned earlier, do their actions match their words? Do they have the passion and drive to teach you how to play Checkers really well or how to play Chess if that's what you want? Just as you probably wouldn't hire an out-of-shape personal trainer, you don't want a financial advisor who isn't financially successful. They don't have to be the Mr.

Olympia of Finance—they just have to implement the strategies they are advising for wealth building.

3. ***How much do you want to be involved?*** Some people are hands-off investors, which is not what I advise if you want to play Chess. The game of Chess is one of strategy, of constantly looking several moves down the board to get you where you want to be. You can't do that by sitting on the sidelines. It's highly improbable that you can hire a bunch of people, tell them, "Go make me wealthy," and have that work out while you're sitting in a lawn chair. When I hire experts, I don't want them to ask me what I want to do. I want them to ask what I want to achieve and then tell me how they will help me reach that end result. When you hire an expert, you shouldn't be hiring an employee who needs instructions.

4. ***What problems are you solving?*** If you invest in a business or industry, like Philip Frost, success comes with solving the problems other people have. Are you filling a gap in the housing market by providing affordable rental properties? Investing in a business that is desperately needed in that demographic? Buying a business that will always be in demand? And do you have the knowledge to invest in this? If not, go get the knowledge.

> To me, wealth is peace of mind. It's time with my family. It's freedom. It's choice.

You don't have to be on *Forbes'* top-ten list to master the strategies in this book. All you need to do is think like the wealthy. Bezos, Musk, Gates—these guys have very little taxable income because they mastered the game of borrowing to buy assets, creating a cash flow that pays back the loans. They make choices that have inherent tax advantages and learn how to deliver what the world needs. They use those choices to build their wealth and attain the ultimate Checkmate.

NOBODY DOES IT ALONE

Even with the information in this book, it can be tough to get to a position of wealth if you try to do it on your own. As I touched on earlier in the book, you're going to need a team, including a financial advisor and tax professional who actually employ the wealth strategies to help you grow your bottom line, too.

In my opinion, the problem is that those kinds of financial advisors are almost as rare as billionaires. In my experience as a wealth advisor, there is a noticeable gap in our industry's approach to assisting clients in building lasting wealth. While we excel at recommending investment options and helping our clients manage risks through insurance products, there is a Grand Canyon-sized hole in helping clients actively create true wealth.

The standard model of how to do things often positions financial advisors as overseers of existing wealth, leaving the onus of creating substantial financial growth largely on the individual. Instead of being proactive architects of wealth creation, advisors can sometimes find themselves primarily being reactive and responding to clients' pre-established financial situations.

I firmly believe that financial advisors should evolve into becoming more collaborative partners who actively contribute to turning their clients' dreams into financial realities. This shift goes beyond the traditional role of safeguarding assets; it involves becoming guides, actively exploring new opportunities, and collectively devising innovative strategies for continuous and meaningful wealth growth.

It's about having the conversations about dreaming beyond retirement and creating generational wealth. It's about talking to clients about life satisfaction, not just dollars and cents. It's also about changing their mindset—and yours.

WORK WITH CHESS PLAYERS

If you wanted to learn how to play a game, you probably wouldn't seek instruction from someone who had never played that game before. They'd make a terrible teacher. It's the same with building wealth: If you want to play Chess, you have to talk to and learn from a Chess player. Checkers players are probably not going to have the advice you need, so be on the lookout for a financial advisor who is a proponent of playing Chess.

Your financial advisor doesn't have to be a billionaire, they simply need to have the kind of financial acumen you are looking to gain. They should be someone to look up to financially.

Don't be afraid to go to brokercheck.finra.org to see what licenses your financial advisor actually has or to do your due diligence by interviewing them. Ask them if they are captive (meaning they can only sell one company's products) or independent financial advisors. Ask them if they have any conflicts of interest (those don't necessarily have to be a bad thing). In my opinion, most financial advisors will have some kind of conflict of interest so find out what they are and how to work best together. Always, always, ask them if they are fiduciaries, which means they are responsible to act in your best interests *every single time*.

As you sit in your first meeting with that financial advisor, weigh what they say to you. Are they pushing products or helping you understand concepts? Are they acting like collaborative partners or salespeople?

Some of their concepts will probably involve some products and/or market-based assets, and that's okay, but it should not be made up entirely of those. When you build a house, you need a certain number of tools to do the job, but when you're done, you want to have a beautiful, actual home, not a really well-stocked toolbox. Spreading your financial choices among different asset classes can be a good strategy.

You want a financial advisor who talks to you about what your goals are, especially if that is about building long-lasting, generational wealth. You don't necessarily need a money manager; you probably do need a visionary and advocate for your financial well-being. That means your financial advisor needs to be proactive and collaborative, working with you toward your personal goals. It's not about simply maintaining your wealth—but rather continuously building upon it so you can achieve your financial aspirations and leave a lasting legacy.

My opinion? If you want to be the next person with the house on Star Island all the tourists talk about (and don't have the scientific acumen to create another Viagra), the best way to get there is by constantly upping your Chess game and finding other players who help you continually raise the bar.

If you'll be perfectly happy playing Checkers and not living on Star Island (or anywhere near it), that's okay, too. Not everyone has to want the same dreams or have the same goals. Decide what yours are and make the moves that get you there.

> Whether you are laughing on your own yacht or laughing at a backyard barbecue, the important thing is laughing because you are happy, no matter where you are.

It's highly unlikely you'll see overnight results, and missteps are pretty much unavoidable, but there is a path to get from where you are right now to where you want to be. You just have to know how to find it, which is what I hope this book will be for you—a preliminary guide to your ultimate financial destination.

"It is not a move, even the best move, that you must seek, but a realizable plan."

– Eugene Znosko-Borovsky

CHAPTER NINE

DON'T DRINK AND INVEST

When I get to heaven, I owe Kobe Bryant a massive apology. When he was playing for the Lakers, I didn't like him. In fact, I didn't like much about him at all. When I first saw him, I thought it was disrespectful for him to have sunglasses perched on his head when he announced his candidacy for the NBA. I thought he was irritating and overly confident on and off the court. Not to mention, he wasn't playing for my favorite team so I had to hold that against him, too.

However, after Bryant tragically died in 2020 when he was just forty-one years old, the news was full of reports about Bryant. They talked about more than his NBA career. They talked about his crazy work ethic and how hard he drove himself in everything he did, from playing on the court to his multiple businesses that he threw himself into after he retired in 2016. I read a book called *Relentless*, written by Kobe

Bryant's trainer, Tim S. Grover, that provided a great outsider view of Bryant's character. I listened to his older speeches about getting better by outworking everyone around him. He was inspiring and smart, and I found his advice to be so great that I started sending clips of his wisdom to my son. Now I'm fully on board with the Mamba Mentality.

Most people who are great at whatever they do—baseball, hockey, technology—have similar attitudes and approaches. For the most part, they didn't spend their earnings in a Gucci store. They kept their head down, worked hard, and kept on making small moves that added up and got really big results. They were not in it for the Maseratis (even if they drove one)—they wanted to be the absolute best at what they did. Even after they reached what they perceived to be the pinnacle, they kept on striving to be better and better at the next thing.

However, when you first start seeing some rewards for all your hard work, it can be pretty tempting to crack open a bottle of Macallan 30-year single malt and celebrate. After a few glasses of scotch, it can also become pretty tempting to go buy whatever you see so you can start enjoying the fruits of your labor. More is more, right? Not really.

It doesn't always work like that. It's extremely easy to get in over your head if you move too fast. You must be smart and methodical.

Becoming wealthy is not an overnight thing. Wealth is built dollar by dollar, investment by investment. You need to have a game plan and not steer away from it because you got seduced by some shiny object.

There are plenty of shiny objects out there. Dozens of seminars on how to get rich quick, influencers claiming they're making millions every year by recording one-minute videos, etc. That get-rich-quick path can look really attractive, but you have to learn how to cut through the BS and do your research. Know when you're being sold a stake in a snake oil company and steer clear of that path.

This "deal" could be in the form of some kind of MLM (Multi-Level Marketing) company. Not that all MLMs are bad…but a lot of them are. MLMs are a business that has minimal capital risk (meaning startup costs), however, so there is something to be said for that.

> If you can't develop a sizable income from simply selling the product or service, then it's probably a pyramid scheme. Move on.

Sometimes all you see is a pretty façade, like a Hollywood set with nothing behind it. Look at the numbers of people who are "wealthy," too, because not all of them live the life they are selling. I've met a lot of realtors who talk about how successful they are, but when you ask them how many houses they sold last year, that number is very low. I'm not picking on realtors, but a lot of people who sell property don't own much of it. When I've asked some of them, "How many doors do you own?" the answer is usually one, or worse, none. I like working with realtors who want to play Chess.

Yes, having a great job or being a successful small business owner can bring in a good income. At the same time, just because you have a successful business doesn't mean you're wealthy. Although it can happen, in general, it's unlikely you will become wealthy from owning a single business or a single piece of property. If you can invent a killer app that all smartphones use, well, that might bring you a whole lot of money, but good luck with that.

Even as a wealth advisor, it's unlikely I would have enough clients investing with me to make me, as the advisor, wealthy from just the fees. That's why I'm always playing Chess with other things, like properties and small businesses, as well as the market.

WHAT YOU DO WITH THE MONEY MATTERS

So, if the business alone is unlikely to make you wealthy, what will? Simple: what you do with the *revenue* the business makes. Chess players know they can take that revenue and multiply their income streams simply by using their money to buy other businesses and properties, as well as purchasing market-based assets that will deliver additional regular income. Again, remember that lenders love to see you do that. These types of investments create income that will keep coming into your bank account long after you decide to stop punching a time card.

If you've started your own business, there's going to come a day when you want to retire. For many entrepreneurs, they are the business. They have a specific skillset or knowledge that basically powers the whole business. When the owner retires, there's not much of a business left. However, if you buy evergreen businesses that continue to run no matter who owns it (like laundromats or a coffee franchise), then those businesses can be transferred or sold when you retire. If the owner of my local Dunkin' Donuts retires or passes away, it doesn't matter to me, the consumer. The business will keep selling coffee every morning. Essentially, you want to have a company where your leaving the business will not make much, if any, difference to the bottom line.

> You have to think of the business as the vehicle that gets you from where you are to where you want to be.

Just like an investment account or property, a business can give you the leverage/reserves you need to take out loans that will buy other things that will increase your cash flow. It's not the single business that creates the wealth; it's the *collective* investments you have.

Think of it like a snowball. Your first piece of property or your first business forms the fist-sized snowball. When you push it down the hill by using your initial investment to purchase other things that increase cash flow, and then do that over and over again, the snowball gets bigger and bigger and gives you more and more leverage, opportunities, and money.

You don't have to sell everything you own (or anything that you own, frankly) to get that giant snowball. If you have one property or one business that generates a ton of income, don't get rid of it because you, in essence, are killing the golden goose. Hold onto it and use that money to invest in the market or take out loans to buy something else.

THERE IS NO RIGHT TREND

Lots of people get tempted to jump on the bandwagon of whatever the hot new thing is. The problem is no one really knows what that is. Before Google, there was Ask Jeeves and Netscape. Who remembers those two? Probably not a lot of people under forty. Neither of those companies saw Google coming, and if you had put all your eggs into the basket of the first search engine you ever used, you would have entirely missed out on Google. All of those companies use the same technology of web crawling, but only one dominated the market. Unless you have a crystal ball, you can't predict which company will be the next Google and which will be the next AltaVista.

You should have a little of what your grandmother might have called pin money—meaning money that you can spend on things that may never return that investment. Money that you can afford to lose, and it won't break you. If you have that and a company like Amazon Web Services (AWS) comes along, offering essentially a toll road system for the digital world, then by all means invest a little in that. Just be on the lookout for the next AWS competitor who could very well upset the entire market and come out ahead.

Your main investments should be in things that are proven, over time, to work. People will always need a place to live. They will always need to wash their clothes. They will always need to educate their kids. Those are things that people have needed from the beginning of time and will continue to need in the foreseeable future. Those are the places where your risks are at least lower.

Right now, people are talking about AI this and AI that. While I'm confident Artificial Intelligence is here to stay, no one really knows who the biggest winner in that tech war will be. If you don't believe me, just think about the last new technology that was introduced—like cell phones—and how the market dramatically changed. Nokia and Motorola no longer dominate the cell phone market. The company with a fruit logo does, along with a company that was known for its entertainment equipment, Samsung.

THE PROOF IS IN THE RESULTS

I know some people like to see the numbers, so let's look at the math for where a million dollars could get you, if you think about growing your wealth differently than you have probably been conditioned to think about investing. Again, these are rough numbers being used for illustration purposes. Real life can look a lot differently:

> **Scenario One, Checkers Playing:** You invest your $1,000,000 in a relatively successful market-based, diversified account that grows at an 8% interest rate that compounds yearly for 10 years. After 10 years, your investment grows to about $2,158,925.

> **Scenario Two, Chess Playing:** You break up that million dollars and put $800,000 in the same investment account with the same 8% interest rate compounding yearly, which grows to about $1,727,140 after 10 years. At the same time, you use the remaining $200,000 as a downpayment for a $1,000,000 property, borrowing $800,000 with a 30-year mortgage at a 7% fixed interest rate.

Let's say that property appreciates with a 4% annual return, which grows to a worth of about $1,480,244 after 10 years. You will then have $793,745 in equity in the property.

Additionally, let's say you cash flowed, after expenses, $5,000 a month from that property, and you reinvested those funds back into your market-based investment account. That will create an additional $900,621, bringing your total amount in your investment account to $2,627,761.

Now, let's combine the market-based investment account with the equity in the real estate investment. When you do that, you get a total of $3,421,506, which beats out Scenario One by $1,262,581. All of this was created by not using *any* more money from your pocket than the original million dollars.

Think about it: You made an additional *$1.2 million dollars* using Scenario Two instead of Scenario One. Now this is with a real estate investment that has generally accepted, conservative numbers and an investment account that delivers realistic returns. In a real-world situation, it could look a lot differently and maybe even *better*, depending on interest rates, capital appreciations, and market returns. Plus, in the real world, you could be taking some of that $5k a month in cash flow and enjoy your life with it.

The Chess strategy of Scenario Two is a concept that a lot of financial advisors miss, for a lot of reasons, whether that's a lack of understanding or simply because they don't want to give up the fees they'll make for the money that is under their management.

Logic says, however, if the client and I can build income streams from other sources, then we are able to keep *more* money under the firm's management because it doesn't get drawn down at high rates to cover the client's income needs. That's a win all around.

So, in simple terms, the second scenario with the split investment, property rental income, and property value ends up being *significantly* more valuable than just investing $1,000,000 outright in the first scenario. And this advice is coming from the guy who's going to make less money from management fees in the second scenario. That's because I know firsthand how great Scenario Two can work out for you.

THE GAME ISN'T RIGGED

I've heard plenty of people say, "Oh that guy got rich because he picked the right stock." Yes, there are some people who bought Apple early on and held onto their shares, but the percentage of people who have amassed their wealth solely from stocks isn't big. In fact, 10% of the people in the world own 93% of all stocks. Only 1% of the people who have invested in stocks have made it really, really big through their market investments.[19] Even so, they aren't solely in the market. If you read that article from the Institute for Policy Studies[20],

---

19 https://ips-dc.org/the-richest-1-percent-own-a-greater-share-of-the-stock-market-than-ever-before/

20 https://inequality.org/great-divide/stock-ownership-concentration/

it explains that those same people "have so much accumulated wealth that their assets are diversified over multiple asset-classes, such as real estate, direct [business] ownership, impact investments, crypto, art, jewelry," etc.

Just like a real-life Chess game, the wealth Chess game doesn't have one single strategy for playing it. If you talk to wealthy people and ask them how they built their wealth, their strategies will all be slightly different. One may be more weighted to residential real estate, another may be into commercial properties, and yet another might own multiple businesses. What you will find in common is their beliefs on how true wealth is amassed.

Essentially, they all agree that ice cream is amazing but may disagree on which flavor is best. If you listen to these people talk, they will echo each other or have common themes in their stories, just like Kobe Bryant's hard work Mamba Mentality philosophy is similar to the one that many, many successful athletes have used to be at the top of their game.

I recently took my son to a Monster Truck Jam in Tampa. The emcee interviewed several of the drivers about what made them so successful in the world of monster trucks, and I heard the same philosophies that people like Kobe Bryant, Michael Jordan, Oprah Winfrey, Derek Jeter, Warren Buffet, Elon Musk, and Jeff Bezos have espoused: hard work, dedication, patience, and perseverance. If you want to get wealthy, essentially, you gotta think like a Monster Truck Jam driver.

I once had a conversation with a realtor about a particular property. I was explaining some of these investment strategies to him and he asked, "Who has the money to do that?"

I replied, "Chess players."

I went on to tell him Chess players put in a lot of hard work, are dedicated to the long-term plan, know that patience will pay off, and keep persevering no matter what because they know they can reach their goal(s).

There are sacrifices you must be willing to make early on in the process, whether that's waiting to buy a nicer house or a new car, because you have a bigger, long-range vision. You may still be working eight hours a day to pay your bills, but using that ninth hour to go after your dreams.

If you're waiting to start doing this, stop. In my opinion, there will never be a "perfect" time to start on this journey. Just as there's never a perfect time for getting married, having kids, or moving to a new state. You just do it and figure it out. Waiting for the right time to start will only get you closer to your headstone.

In fact, today is a much better time than ever before because the access to information is available to anyone. You can learn a lot of what you need to know in classes, books, and on the Internet.

Go buy that business or that property. You don't need a master's degree to make those moves. When my kids were little, my wife and I watched YouTube videos on Christmas

Eve so we could assemble the kids' toys before Santa put them under the tree. If we can learn how to assemble a complicated remote-control car from a YouTube video, you can learn how to become wealthy with the information already at your fingertips.

BUT WHAT IF I FAIL?

You don't need to hit a home run every time you buy something or invest in something. The truth is, you *won't* hit a home run every time—and that's okay. Some ideas simply don't work, for whatever reason. Even for me, I'll have an idea that fails and, a decade later, I'm still not sure why it didn't work. Could have been timing, could have been something else. Who knows?

In my opinion, your best bet to avoid failure is to choose the boring things. Boring stuff can be great. I love boring. I love boring rates of return, boring businesses, boring pieces of real estate. Boring can create a good amount of wealth. You don't have to invest in every exciting thing that comes along. You can just keep doing the boring, dependable moves that pay off well in the end.

> The key is to make smart, strategic moves, like the best Chess players do. Impetuous, irrational moves are very unlikely to pay off in the end.

If you don't make a billion dollars or fifty million—or whatever your dream number is—it doesn't mean you are a failure. Once you get to a certain level of wealth, when your bottom line shows more money than you ever thought you were going to have, everything else will likely become immaterial. You don't care if you trade in the Chevy for the Maserati because life with the Chevy is pretty damned good.

When I was much younger and struggling, I remember wanting to buy a shirt from Banana Republic. It seemed like such an extravagant purchase at the time. One day, I walked into a Banana Republic store with my non-fashionista friend. It was the first time he'd been in one of those stores and he said, "This place even *smells* expensive."

However, once I got to the level of wealth where I could afford a shirt from Banana Republic (or Armani), I realized I didn't care what the label said. I'm just as happy in a plain old, boring T-shirt.

That's why I talked earlier in this book about deciding what kind of *life* you are looking to build. If you dream of living in a house on the beach and making five million dollars gives you enough wealth to do that, then I'd say you were a success. If you dream of retiring at fifty and having enough time and money to travel the world, then you're a success. It's your definition, not mine.

> Your Chess game can be whatever level you want it to be. Maybe you don't want to manage a hundred properties or a bunch of businesses. That is totally okay. Only take on what allows you to still have a life you love.

I was recently at a mastermind event where the roundtable discussion was about achieving a work-life balance. There were several people who had high revenue numbers, but the sacrifices they made in their lives in order to achieve those numbers wasn't worth it for them. I want to build my wealth but still have a personal life because I'm literally doing this in order to have that life. I can manage my businesses and do my real estate deals during the week, and if I want to take off and head to Steinbrenner Field and watch the Yankees play a spring training game in the middle of the afternoon, I can.

To me, there are more important things in life than money.

"One of the principal requisites of good chess is the ability to treat both middle and end game equally well."

—Aron Nimzowitsch

CHAPTER TEN

THE ULTIMATE CHECKMATE

Checkmate.

Game over (or maybe just beginning). If you're a Chess player, that's your goal from the beginning of the game to its end. In the world of building wealth, reaching Checkmate isn't about destroying your opponent (or anyone else); it's about finding that place that gives you the most happiness and life satisfaction, which I hope you have defined by now or else you're going to be chasing something as elusive as clouds.

DEFINING CHECKMATE

In my opinion, reaching Checkmate (from a financial perspective) is all about being able to borrow whatever amount of money you need to buy assets that can create passive income while avoiding creating taxable events, which ultimately keeps more of the money in your pocket and in your Chess game. The typical mindset of capital appreciation is to buy low and sell high, but what I like better is buying, borrowing, and dying...Well, not the dying part; but we all know it's inevitable, and it'd be nice to not die broke and leaving wealth to the next generation. Checkmate isn't about selling—it's about keeping as many of your pieces on the board as you can to win the game.

When you play Chess, you typically focus on growing your own wealth, not someone else's. However, most Chess games do benefit someone or something else, like the bank. The money you borrow to buy a rental property, for instance, results in interest income for the bank, which then invests that income into their corporate Chess plan.

The big numbers often flow in the direction of the one making the most from that investment—and you want that to be you. Remember, all the other Chess players out there (myself included) are the ones standing behind you in line at that bank ready to borrow the money you just deposited and using that borrowed money to create more income for ourselves. Thanks for that!

Wouldn't it be better to put those earnings into your pocket? The strategies outlined in this book should help you do that.

I don't want you to think you shouldn't have any money in the bank. Just know what the Chess player strategy is as you're making your financial decisions.

It doesn't matter whether you choose to get to Checkmate through rental properties or businesses (or both), or any of the other tax-saving, income-earning strategies we talked about in these chapters. No matter which you choose, you should always look ahead to the next move, and the one after that, until you get to the wealth level that makes you feel satisfied.

There will always be the temptation to put it all on black and go all in with whatever works for you. I advise against that because diversification is what will help you ride out whatever economic shifts come about. The numbers I've shown you in this book give evidence to that theory over and over again.

MONEY DOESN'T BUY HAPPINESS; IT'S ONLY A DOWN PAYMENT

The old adage about "money solves all problems" is only partially true. It does help make life a lot easier, yes, but it doesn't necessarily work as a panacea for everything in your life. More money doesn't necessarily make your outcome better. Think about it—if you aren't doing the right things with your money to begin with, how will throwing more money at those decisions change the results?

I like to look at money as a problem solver. It's a slight shift in the mindset, because now you see the money you have as a solution for *other people's problems,* just like Philip Frost did and so many others have before him. People had a problem getting from one place to another quickly, so Henry T. Ford was one of the pioneers of the automobile. People had a problem traveling long distances in their cars and on trains, so the Wright Brothers invented airplanes. The people who invest in or create problem-solvers often become the wealthiest because they have created something others want—and need.

Jeff Bezos is a perfect example of this. When he started Amazon, Bezos only sold books, but he soon saw there was a need for selling other merchandise people couldn't get easily or didn't want to drive to go buy. He has made billions of dollars thinking about the problems people have and creating solutions (Groceries delivered? Check. Prescriptions delivered? Check. Movies, music, ebooks delivered instantly (especially this one!)? Check, check, check). Like I mentioned earlier, he made a ton of money by building digital toll roads on the Internet with Amazon Web Services. He solved a cost problem for other companies by building an infrastructure they needed.

You don't have to be Jeff Bezos to achieve Checkmate, especially your version of Checkmate. Personally, I don't want to rule the world; it sounds like a lot of headaches.

YOU MAY NOT FIND WHAT YOU NEED IN YOUR BACKYARD

A lot of people buy their first properties in an area close to where they live. Much of the time, I advise against this because of something called the cap rate, also known as the capitalization rate. This is a real estate valuation measure that helps investors analyze the property, especially when it comes to potential risks. An up-and-coming area, for instance, will likely have a higher cap rate than an established, more desirable neighborhood, just because the established neighborhood is already one that people want to live in.

Where you live is very likely a place that's attractive to other people just like you. The prices are probably high, and the cap rate is probably low. Which means it'll be much harder for you to increase the cash flow on your investment than it would be if you bought a property in a place with a higher cap rate. With a low cap rate, the price will likely be too high and the rent you could receive will be too low to make much of a profit, if at all. Just because the cap rate is high doesn't mean it couldn't be a great deal.

For example, in early 2019, I was buying properties in Jacksonville, FL. I had researched the area and saw that the housing prices were reasonable, the rents were good, and the cap rate was at a good level for me, all signs that properties there would have a positive cash flow.

Then a real estate boom—more like an explosion—happened in Florida as people who could now work from home moved to the Sunshine State in droves (Pinellas County alone had 10,000 new residents move in per month for many months).

Suddenly, the prices went up, and I could see that anything else I bought in that area would have a much lower cash flow.

The prices got so high that the numbers didn't make sense for investing, so I started researching other areas, far from the real estate boom in Florida.

When a secret gets out about a particular market, it can change everything. Maybe you're interested in buying an entire block of properties. You buy the first two houses on that street, but then the neighborhood improves (which is ultimately a good thing), and suddenly, all the houses in that neighborhood go up in value and price. The downside? Chances are, rent rates didn't rise so your cash flow with each subsequent purchase may shrink.

So how do you choose the right location to buy in? I like the 1% rule, meaning 1% of the purchase price should be around the amount for rent you can get for that property. If I buy a $200,000 house, then rents in that area should be about $2000 a month. If they're much lower, I won't likely see positive cash flow on my investment. The name of the game in real estate is cash flow.

As I write this book, it's more difficult to find 1% properties because interest rates and prices are higher at the moment, but rent isn't keeping pace with those numbers. It's not impossible to find a 1% deal, it just means you need to be willing to hop around and look at different areas. If that property is many hours away from you or in another state, no problem. Simply hire a good property manager to take care of that for you.

I encourage people to use a property management service to avoid trying to do it all themselves. Remember, we're trying to create more money—and more time to enjoy that money.

WHAT ABOUT AIRBNB AND FLIPPING?

A lot of people ask me, *Can I just Airbnb my rental property?* Yes, you can, and in some highly desirable vacation areas, you can have great results. Vacation properties, however, are affected by vacation trends. The market can also be easily flooded by people who think it's an easy path to riches. One location may be the place to vacation in this year, and next year the hot spot could be in another area, even another state. Look at the risk and reward of a property in that area before deciding to make it a vacation rental.

This, in my opinion, is the kind of thing that looks really good until you do it because the market can flood easily in a "hot" spot. I'm not saying don't do vacation rentals, just be very, very cautious because this can be a real estate siren leading you to your doom.

Flipping is when you buy a property (hopefully) cheap, renovate it, and get it back on the market as fast as possible. In my opinion, this is like being a waiter or waitress of real estate. You have to move fast, work hard, and hope to make fast cash. In the long run, it is a very hard path toward building wealth.

The problem arises when the market turns on you, which can happen quickly. Prices can skyrocket, interest rates can rise, or desire for a particular area can plummet. Interest rates, access to capital, how quickly you can sell the house, all play a big part in your potential success. When interest rates soared to 7% in 2023, houses probably sat on the market a lot longer or sold at a lower price than they did when rates were at 2%. Flipping is likely to be considered active or earned income which comes with a possibly higher tax bill, especially if you are doing it part-time and it's adding to your already-earned W-2 income.

Cheapening the flip can also backfire. To make a profit, many flippers buy basic cabinets, basic flooring, etc., which can lower the asking price and the potential buyer pool. It could be a good way to get into real estate investing overall but, in my opinion, you'll likely be kicking yourself at some point for selling those properties to someone like me who will hold onto them and earn regular income from the rent. This is called the "buy and hold" strategy.

HOW TO ACHIEVE CHECKMATE

When you start making money, I know it will be tempting to spend it, especially if you've been working hard and saving for a while. Wait. Don't spend it yet. You don't want to immediately increase your lifestyle to match your income for several reasons: It's easy to make a misstep early on and lose some money. To keep leveling up, you need to have reserves, and spending that money won't necessarily make you happier.

Ironically, as I was writing this chapter, James Clear, author of *Atomic Habits*, sent out his weekly newsletter. In it, he wrote, "Don't sacrifice peace of mind for a piece of luxury." If you spend the money too quickly, you'll put yourself right back in that stressed, paycheck-to-paycheck place you worked so hard to escape. I'm not saying not to buy the luxuries at all, just buy them when your passive or recurring income allows you to easily afford it.

You don't have to wait forever to spend your hard-earned money. Just wait as long as it takes to play a good Chess game. Don't think of these (possibly) few years of waiting to spend as sacrifices, but as investments that will have long-term payoffs. It really might not take as long as you think to get there.

Some of us are just as happy with a $10 bottle of wine as we are with one that costs $100. The ones who drink the $10 bottle of wine have $90 more to invest in their future than the ones who drink the more expensive blend. This is an analogy you can use for basically all indulgences or things that make life more enjoyable—cars, vacations, whatever. If you are still growing and investing, consider whether that luxury purchase is something you really care about and whether it's the best choice for the plans you have.

And if you enjoy expensive wine, drink the cheap stuff now so you can play Chess and later afford all the expensive wine you want. Don't deprive yourself of all wine—just buy the reasonably-priced bottles.

YOUR EXIT STRATEGY COULD BE NEVER, EVER SELL

Level up when you're ready to take on more responsibility and investments. I usually advise people to start small and work their way up to multiple properties in a portfolio. You want your growth to be manageable so you aren't constantly stressed or pressured to make decisions. As you grow, you can hire a team for a lot of the analysis, purchase, and management tasks; but early on, chances are you'll be doing all those things yourself.

Your goal is to get to the point where you have minimal involvement, you're not so hands-on, and you have hired a team you trust. This team can consist of a financial advisor, a tax professional, an insurance person, a realtor, a lender, and a property manager, just to name a few.

Then you sit and hold onto what you have. True Checkmate comes with basically never, ever selling. I mean it. Never, ever.

Every time you even think about selling, I want you to think about the Mickey Mantle baseball card story. The story goes: There was a guy who owned an original, mint condition, 1952 Mantle baseball card. He sold it at auction for millions of dollars. As he walked away from the auction with several million dollars in his pocket, someone asked him how he felt. He said he was sad because his journey with that card, which had been with him for years and through a lot of major events and moves he'd made, was now over.

I was frustrated with him for another reason. I read the article and screamed at this guy (who couldn't hear me or he might have made a different decision), "Why did you freaking sell the card? You could have used it as collateral to buy cash-flowing investments, like a great property, that would pay you every single month!" Now, not only does the guy own no property to increase his cash flow, he likely owes *a lot* of capital gains taxes on the millions he just made. And he no longer owns the 1952 Mantle card, one of the biggest treasures in all of baseball card collecting, second only to Honus Wagner (which was briefly produced in 1909 by a tobacco company; one of those sold for more than $7 million in 2020).

People with considerable wealth buy things like art. Art doesn't fluctuate as much in value as other things so it stores value more easily. A million dollars in a briefcase requires a huge briefcase whereas a Picasso on the wall doesn't take up much room. Plus, you get to hang it on your wall while leveraging it to buy properties that *pay* for those walls (and your lifestyle).

If you hold onto the property, stocks, or baseball cards you own until you pass away, it will go to your heirs as an asset, which then puts them in a position to use it as reserves/collateral to borrow against. Now they have the leverage to borrow along with a step-up in basis for tax purposes, and they can buy properties and create *more* cash flow. Estate planning may require liquidity for state tax purposes but that's a topic for another book. Either way, the great thing about this kind of Checkmate is that it can be in place in perpetuity.

When that happens, you and your heirs have time to work on that great invention idea you had or start that business you always dreamed of creating, or heck, go be the best circus clown in the world, if that's your passion.

At its core, Checkmate really is...freedom.

"These young guys are playing checkers.
I'm out there playing chess."

– Kobe Bryant

ACKNOWLEDGMENTS

First, for my mom and dad (Fred and Phyllis): I want to express my deepest gratitude for the incredible examples of hard work and sacrifice you've set throughout your lives. Dad, as an electrician, and Mom, as a waitress, your dedication to making sacrifices has paved the way for me to attend exceptional schools like St. Anthony's High School on Long Island and Belmont Abbey College in North Carolina.

Your strategic game of Checkers, starting from where we lived in Queens and diligently working and saving, ensured I had opportunities for a quality education. The secure mindset you instilled in me to listen to the advice of more financially successful individuals and explore different paths has proven to be invaluable.

While your grandchildren understand the importance of a strong work ethic, they won't experience the same struggles you endured. Instead of playing Checkers, they'll play Chess, benefiting from the foundation you helped build. We are now in the process of building generational wealth, and each succeeding generation will have even greater opportunities than the one before.

Thank you for your unwavering commitment to our family's success. Your resilience and foresight have set us on a path toward a brighter and more prosperous future.

To one of the first Chess players I ever met, Dave Vitalis: You have been like a "Rich Dad" to me. Your extremely blunt and unapologetic attitude towards your wealth was exactly what I needed to hear in my early 20s. It wasn't just about the money, but the confidence and straightforwardness with which you approached success that truly resonated with me. You didn't sugarcoat the realities of achieving financial success, and that raw honesty inspired me to pursue my goals with a similar mindset. Your influence has been invaluable, shaping not only my approach to playing Chess but also my attitude towards life and success. Thank you for being a pivotal figure in my journey.

To my wife Barb: I want to take a moment to express my deepest gratitude for your unwavering support throughout all of the ventures and challenges we've faced together. Your strength and patience have been my anchor.

I know it wasn't easy for you during the years when I was serving as a cop. The long hours, the unpredictability, and the inherent risks of the job must have been both frustrating and worrisome. Yet, you stood by me with grace and resilience, managing everything on the home front and being my pillar of strength.

When I decided to start the firm, you once again showed your incredible support. Starting a business is never easy, and balancing it with my duties as a cop meant even longer hours and greater demands on our time. Despite this, you encouraged me, believed in me, and were there every step of the way. Your belief in my abilities gave me the confidence to push through the challenges.

Now, as our Chess game gains momentum and success, I am thrilled that we can finally look forward to spending more time together, doing the things we enjoy. This new chapter brings with it the promise of shared moments, laughter, and the simple joys that we sometimes had to put on hold.

Barb, your support and love have been the bedrock of my journey. I am deeply thankful for everything you've done and continue to do. Here's to us, to our shared dreams, and to all the wonderful moments ahead.

With heartfelt appreciation,

—Freddie

ABOUT THE AUTHOR

When Freddie Rappina was working in law enforcement for the Fairfax County Police Department in Virginia, he realized he needed to do more than just invest in a retirement plan if he wanted to provide his family with generational wealth. After retiring from the force, he dedicated himself to studying the world of finance, focusing on what the wealthy and mega-corporations do to amass their financial fortunes.

If you're ready to start making strategic financial moves, schedule a consultation with Freddie at calendly.com/freddierappina

Made in the USA
Middletown, DE
22 August 2024